Fasting in the New Testament

Theological Inquiries

Studies in Contemporary
Biblical and Theological Problems

General Editor
Lawrence Boadt, C. S. P.

PAULIST PRESS
New York • Ramsey • Toronto

Fasting in the New Testament

A Study in Biblical Theology

Joseph F. Wimmer, O.S.A.

PAULIST PRESS
New York • Ramsey • Toronto

Library of Congress
Catalog Card Number: 81-83183

ISBN: 0-8091-2420-3

Published by Paulist Press
545 Island Road, Ramsey, N.J. 07446

Printed and bound in the
United States of America

Contents

to my parents
Joseph and Johanna Wimmer

Introduction

After a period of decline in recent years, fasting is gaining new momentum. The renewed interest in fasting has given rise to a relatively large body of current literature on the subject. Most of these books and articles include a consideration of biblical texts from the Old and New Testaments, but the passages are often merely cited and treated superficially, and not rarely from a fundamentalistic point of view.

At the same time professional biblical studies have become highly complex, with an emphasis on the historico-critical, and now redactional, methods of research, and have given insufficient attention to the hermeneutical aspects of their work. The reader is often disappointed in their conclusions, for they seem to offer little by way of guidelines for the present. One is almost tempted to by-pass these complex studies in an effort to simply "let the Bible speak for itself."

It is this situation that has occasioned the present study of the New Testament texts on fasting from both a critical and a hermeneutical point of view, in an attempt to provide a solid biblical base for our understanding of fasting today. What is the meaning of fasting according to the New Testament? Is there really such a thing as "Christian" fasting? What would be its characteristics? What was the practice of Jesus and his disciples? Of the apostolic Church? Is it normative for us? To what extent?

To my knowledge there is no extensive study on fasting that considers all the New Testament texts in the light of contemporary literary criticism and hermeneutics in order to arrive at a synthesis of the Christian biblical teaching on fasting. This work is meant to fill that gap.

METHOD

After a brief consideration of hermeneutics, followed by a historical survey of fasting in the milieu of Jesus and of Hellenism, each of the most important New Testament texts on fasting is treated with the aid of form criticism from a threefold point of view:

1. its function in the redaction in which it appears;
2. its place in the kerygma of the apostolic community, especially as indicated by its literary genre and *Sitz im Leben;*
3. its relationship to the historical Jesus insofar as this can be determined.

I have found it best to begin with the second level, that of the oral and written tradition behind the Gospels. This process involves a double step: the text of the tradition must be isolated from its context (and possible transformation) in the redaction, but in order to do this, the redactional elements must be clearly recognized. Once the traditional material is isolated, it can then be questioned as regards its origin by a study of its literary genre and *Sitz im Leben,* and we should be able to see which elements (or passages) derive from the Palestinian Christian community, and which, if any, from the Hellenistic, and, finally, how they relate to the historical Jesus. Short conclusions about the meaning and motivation of fasting are then presented at the end of the individual chapters.

A final section summarizes the conclusions and presents a synthesis of the meaning of fasting for us today, with due consideration for the hermeneutical principles involved.

CHAPTER ONE

Hermeneutics

The classical definition of hermeneutics proposed by Wilhelm Dilthey and accepted by Rudolph Bultmann and many others is still the best: "the art of arriving at the understanding of life expressed in a written text."[1] In terms of the New Testament passages on fasting we are encouraged to search for the insight into life which they contain. This truth can be formulated as a general principle:

> Fasting is an expression of life; a study of the biblical texts which treat of it should disclose to us various aspects of that life.

A further dimension of hermeneutics is brought out by Bernard Lonergan's concept of the mediation of a world by meaning.[2] The world in question is a human one, "a world of language, art . . . of family and mores . . ."; the mediation is an "intentional" one, and meaning is itself considered as a "constitutive component of human living."[3]

As regards fasting, the whole world of associations it has in the New Testament can be mediated to us. This gives us the reality of

---

1. W. Dilthey, "Die Entstehung der Hermeneutik," *Gesammelte Schriften* V (Göttingen: Vandenhoeck & Ruprecht, 1924) 317–338; N. Perrin, "Eschatology and Hermeneutics: Reflections on Method in the Interpretation of the New Testament," *JBL* 93 (1974) 3–14.

2. B. Lonergan, *Method in Theology* (New York: Herder, 1972) 28f, 76f; F.E. Crowe, "The Power of the Scriptures: Attempt at Analysis," *Word and Spirit*, Essays in Honor of D.M. Stanley, ed. by J. Plevnik (Willowdale, Ontario: Regis College Press, 1975) 323–347.

3. Crowe, "Power of the Scriptures," 330–338.

Christian fasting, which is different from other realities such as Buddhist fasting, for it has a different meaning, a different intentionality, a different constitutive component.

Exegetes recognize that the associations connected with a reality form part of its meaning. H. Riesenfeld, for instance, notes that the words and actions of Jesus are charged with associations, not only of daily life in Palestine but even more of religious existence, of the Hebrew Bible with its memories, feelings, ideas, and hopes.[4] The image of the Good Shepherd, for example, has resonances not only in secular experience; it brings to mind many passages from the Old Testament: Ps 23, "The Lord is my shepherd"; Ez 36:11–16, "I will be the shepherd of my sheep . . ."; Gen 49:24; Pss 77:21; 78:52; 79:13; 80:2; 95:7; 100:3; Is 40:11; Jer 23:3; 31:10; Mi 2:12. Similarly, the scene of Jesus fasting forty days in the desert (Mt 4:2) brings with it a host of Old Testament associations which form part of its meaning.

These reflections lead to a second principle:

> Fasting is a human reality, and therefore has a meaning which is one of its constitutive parts. Christian fasting is thus different from other kinds of fasting, but the many associations connected with it also form part of its meaning.

Although it is a concrete act, fasting is also a symbol and is open to an increasingly more profound understanding of reality. Paul Ricoeur considers symbol as a sign with an opaque meaning so that we are led to erect a second intentionality upon the first, and thus proceed by analogy to ever deeper meanings. He says, "The symbol gives rise to thought."[5] Norman Perrin takes this up and applies it to the phrase "kingdom of God" as used in the preaching of Jesus; he shows that as a "true" symbol it leads us "to explore the manifold ways in which the experience of God can become an existential reality to man."[6]

Fasting has a symbolic function and it is capable of allowing a

---

4. H. Riesenfeld, "Le caractère messianique de la tentation au désert," *La venue du Messie,* Recherches Bibliques VI, ed. by E. Massaux (Desclée de Brouwer, 1962) 51–63.

5. P. Ricoeur, *The Symbolism of Evil* (Boston: Beacon Press, 1969) 348.

6. Perrin, "Eschatology and Hermeneutics," 13.

person to penetrate more deeply into an understanding of his/her relationships to self, others, the world, and God.

F. Mussner states[7] that the task of biblical hermeneutics consists in a threefold interpretation: (a) The historical, whereby we use all the philological and historiographical tools available in order to understand the cultural milieu which underlies the text. (b) The existential, based on our present self-understanding, which differs from person to person, e.g., from one who believes in life after death to one who does not. The Bible can help us toward a better self-understanding before God; it calls to us as the word of God and brings light into our life, into its inner turmoil, ambiguity, and lack of direction. It judges our evil deeds and urges us to repentance. (c) The salvation history kerygmatic, an encounter with the definitive presence of God in Christ and the living of a new life in him. Tradition also plays an important role, for it helps determine the pre-understanding with which we approach the biblical text and keeps us from many errors of interpretation.

In terms of the hermeneutic of fasting, Mussner would insist on a form-critical study of the biblical texts in order to understand the practice in its historical setting, then look for the light it throws on our self-understanding, while being aware of the influence and importance of the interpretation of those texts in the Church, through which we are united to God in Christ.

As a third principle we could say:

> The biblical texts on fasting have a symbolic dimension and should bring us to a better self-understanding in all our essential relationships, toward ourselves, others, the world, and God.

The richness of the meaning mediated by a text has been stressed especially by H. G. Gadamer.[8] The point of departure is not the author but the text. In fact, the reader might understand the text

---

7. F. Mussner, "Aufgaben und Ziele der biblischen Hermeneutik," *Praesentia Salutis* (Düsseldorf: Patmos-Verlag, 1967) 9–19.

8. H.-G. Gadamer, *Truth and Method* (New York: Seabury, 1975); S. Schneiders, "Faith, Hermeneutics, and the Literal Sense of Scripture," *TS* 39 (1978) 719–736.

better than the author did himself, for he stands in a tradition which, with the passage of time, has eliminated certain sources of error and discovered new sources of understanding that reveal unsuspected relationships of meaning; as a result the discovery of the true meaning of a text or work of art is an endless process.

In this sense, reading a book is like engaging in a conversation with someone. In a conversation two people try to come to a deeper understanding about a topic of common interest. If they succeed, it is not simply that "B" has correctly understood what "A" had to say, but rather that both have grasped the truth, which might be different from what either originally thought or said. There is of course a difference between a book and a conversational partner, but there is also a similarity, for the book, as a mediation of meaning, confronts the reader and challenges him/her; it calls into play his/her consciousness, "a consciousness which is effectively historically structured and which is, therefore, not identical with that of any other interpreter."[9]

Sandra Schneiders, following the thought of Gadamer, compares the text to a musical composition and states that it "cannot be rendered except by genuine fidelity to the score," but notes at the same time that it will be "rendered differently by each artist."[10] The musical score is the same, but its actualization is different in each case. Indeed, the more capable the musician, the more faithful the rendering, and—paradoxically—the more original. Similarly, the more learned and experienced the reader, the greater will be his/her understanding of the text, and the more personal.

We are now in a position to state the fourth and final principle:

The more profound, experienced, and developed our own personalities, the greater will be our understanding of the true meaning of fasting.

9. Schneiders, 731.
10. *Ibid.*

CHAPTER TWO

Fasting in the Milieu of Jesus and His Times

What were the attitudes and practices regarding fasting in the time of Jesus? What was the general social and religious context within which fasting is to be understood?

Roger Le Dèaut, writing about the source material necessary for a study of Judaism, insists on the abiding importance of the Pentateuch, prophets, and psalms as a "living expression of the piety of Israel."[1] To assess the spiritual climate in the time of Jesus, we must begin with the Hebrew Scriptures, though we must also consult the more recent deutero-canonical works, the apocrypha, and other extra-biblical literature. Greek texts on fasting should also be considered in order to provide a comparison between the Semitic and Hellenistic points of view.

FASTING IN THE OLD TESTAMENT

Fasting may be defined as refraining from eating and drinking out of a religious motive. Complete abstinence from food and water seems to be the fundamental meaning of ṣum, "to fast," both in the Old Testament and in later Jewish tradition. In response to the preaching of Jonah, according to Jon 3:7f, the king of Nineveh decreed: "Let neither man nor beast, herd nor flock, taste anything: let them not feed or drink water." The mourning fast in Ezr 10:6 is described as "neither eating bread nor drinking water"; in Est 4:16 we

---

1. "Judaisme," *Dictionnaire de Spiritualité* VIII, 1488 (1974).

learn that the queen told Mordecai, ". . . hold a fast on my behalf, and neither eat nor drink for three days, night or day." Most of the texts on fasting do not state explicitly that drinking water was also prohibited, but the examples cited above lead us to conclude that such was the case. Fasting in the Old Testament means complete abstinence from food and drink.

Fasting as total absence of food and drink is found also in Acts 9:9, which states that Paul, brought to Damascus immediately after his conversion, was without sight for three days "and neither ate nor drank." It is also the requirement of the public fasts in rabbinic Judaism, especially the Day of Atonement, as seen, for instance, in Mishna Yoma 8,2: "He who eats on the Day of Atonement as much as a big date, that is, as much as the date including its seed, and who drinks as much as his saliva, is guilty."

Ordinary fast days lasted from morning until evening (Jgs 20:26; 1 Sam 14:24; 2 Sam 1:12). In later Judaism the duration of private fasts was regulated by the *halacha;* it was possible to fast for just a certain number of hours. The fast on the Day of Atonement lasted a full day, twenty-four hours (twenty-six in later Judaism), from sundown of the previous evening until after sundown of the day itself (Lev 23:26–32).

The origins of fasting in Israel are lost in antiquity. Fasting was part of the ritual in preparation for waging a holy war (1 Sam 14:24); it was a sign of mourning for the dead (1 Sam 31:13; 2 Sam 1:12; 3:35), and it was particularly important in times of distress.

When the Israelites fasted in reaction to calamity, they did so in order to express a twofold religious attitude: penance and supplication. The penitential aspect of fasting is brought out by the confession of sinfulness which accompanied it (1 Sam 7:6; Neh 9:1–3; Jon 3:8), while its character of appeal is evident in the concomitant prayer of petition (Ezr 8:21–23; Neh 1:4,10f).

The fundamental note of fasting in the Old Testament is humble self-abasement before the Lord. This is shown by the close connection between the expression ṣum, "to fast," and 'innah nephesh, "to humble oneself," as in Ps 35:13, "I humbled myself with fasting"; cf Ps 69:11. The latter expression is used exclusively in the regulations about the Day of Atonement, the strictest fast in Israel: Lev 16:29, 31; 23:27,32; Num 29:7. In Ezr 8:21 we read: "I proclaimed a fast there, at the river Ahava, that we might humble ourselves before God."

The Israelites were aware of the independence of God, and though they might hope that he would be influenced by their penitential fast, as David said so well: "Who knows whether the Lord will be gracious to me, that the child may live?" (2 Sam 12:22), they knew that the source of his divine assistance was his own goodness and gracious, merciful love.

Fasting received a strong impulse after the exile. It is mentioned in Ezr 8:21,23; Neh 1:4; 9:1; 2 Chr 20:3; Bar 1:5; Sir 34:26; 1 Mac 3:47; 2 Mac 13:12. Its importance is emphasized in two popular historical novels, Esther, the cult legend of the feast of Purim which was preceded by a fast, and Judith, a romantic portrayal of the ideal post-exilic widow who "fasted every day of her widowhood" except on the official feast days (8:6), and who, under God's guidance, daringly cut off the head of Holofernes. Both these works have links with the Book of Jonah, precisely as regards the penitential fast of the Ninivites, Jon 3:5–8. All these books—and Daniel too—show the providence of God for his faithful servants, and through them, for Israel; all these servants are characterized by their fasting (Est 4:16; Jdt 8:6; Dan 9:3). Tob 2:4 and 12:13 may also be added to this group.

Particularly instructive about the importance, dangers, and motivation of fasting is the criticism of the prophets, all of them exilic or post-exilic: Jer 14:12; Jl 2:12–14; Zech 7–8; Is 58:1–12. These texts are a call toward inner religious authenticity. Jl 2:12–14 states this explicitly: "Return to me with all your heart, with fasting, with weeping, and with mourning; and rend your hearts and not your garments." Is 58:5–7 includes concern for one's neighbor: ". . . to share your bread with the hungry, and bring the homeless poor into your house; when you see the naked, to cover him. . . ." The relationship between fasting and charity emphasized here prepared the way for the teaching of Mt 6:1–18 on the inner connection between almsgiving, prayer, and fasting.

THE APOCRYPHA

Fasting is mentioned frequently in the Apocrypha, especially in the Testaments of the Twelve Patriarchs. What follows is a brief treatment of the more significant apocryphal texts on fasting that reflect the Jewish religious climate in the time of Jesus.

The Testaments of the Twelve Patriarchs

There is much controversy about the date and place of origin of this work. With caution we may say that it probably originated slightly before the period of the Maccabees, between 200 and 174 B.C., and that it reflects Jewish moral ideals, but it contains later additions, especially Christian interpolations. It is very parenetic in style and may reflect the preaching in the synagogue during the Hellenistic period.[2]

Fasting is presented as a means of overcoming vice. T Sim III,1–6 mentions envy, so strong that it can cause people to stop eating and drinking or doing any good thing. Simeon wanted to overcome this evil and succeeded in doing so by "afflicting" himself with fasting for two years "in the fear of the Lord." III,5 explains the principle involved: "If a man flee to the Lord, the evil spirit will run away from him." Fasting is seen as an act of humbling oneself before God and is tantamount to "fleeing" to him. The need for perseverance is hinted at by the time factor: two years, but it is effective, for the envy went away.

Another example is temptation against chastity. Joseph was tempted by the Egyptian woman, but he "remembered the words" of his father, prayed in his chamber, fasted "in those seven years," and when his master was out, he drank no wine and ate nothing for three days, while giving his bread to the poor and sick. His face became brilliant, as if he were living in luxury, "for they that fast for the sake of God receive beauty of face" (T Jos III,1–5). Still the Egyptian woman persisted, as the embodiment of temptation, and Joseph continued to fast and pray (IV,8). Nevertheless she would not give up, but even in prison Joseph continued to fast, as we can gather from his statement in IX,2: "God loves him better who chastely fasts in a

2. O. Eissfeldt, *The Old Testament: An Introduction* (New York: Harper and Row, 1965) 631–636; M. de Jonge, "The Interpretation of the Testaments of the Twelve Patriarchs in Recent Years," *Studies on the Testaments of the Twelve Patriarchs,* ed. by M. de Jonge (Leiden: Brill, 1975) 183–192.

dark dungeon than the one who gives himself up to lust in the chambers of the kings." X,2 concludes the lesson: "See now, my children, what great things patience and prayer with fasting accomplish." Fasting is considered in conjunction with prayer, almsgiving, patience, perseverance, and a religious motive, "for the sake of God" (III,4). The connection between prayer and fasting is brought out also in T Ben I,4: Rachel was barren for twelve years after giving birth to Joseph, but she prayed and fasted, and then bore Benjamin.

Finally, there is a polemic against fasting while continuing to commit sin, a theme reminiscent of the prophets: T Ash II,8; IV,3.

Penance for sin committed is also treated, but the examples given refer to absention from meat and wine (T Reub I,10, for seven years, for the sin of fornication; T Jud XV,4, "until old age", also for fornication), rather than for fasting as such, though T Jud XIX,2 mentions repentance for greed as consisting in "humiliation" (= fasting?) and the prayers of one's father.

I Enoch (Ethiopian)

This book has one text on fasting, 108,7–9, part of an independent (concluding) chapter which speaks of "the humble, those who have afflicted their bodies and been recompensed by God," those who "longed not after earthly food." The chapter seems to have been written before 63 B.C., perhaps by an Essene.[3] It is ascetical in tone and presents fasting in connection with humility, divine reward, and the idea of heaven; verse 10 goes on to mention God's reward "because they loved heaven more than their life in the world."

Psalms of Solomon

Ps Sol 3:8 declares that the just man "atones involuntary sins through fasting and humbles his (soul)." It is part of a collection of eighteen psalms which come from Palestine, probably Jerusalem, and were used in the cult, perhaps in a synagogue. They were written

---

3. Eissfeldt, "*Introduction*," 619f; A.M. Denis, *Introduction aux pseudépigraphes grecs d'Ancien Testament* (Leiden: Brill, 1970) 27.

about the middle of the first century B.C.[4] The attitude toward fasting is Jewish and includes the concept of atoning for involuntary sins (Lev 4:13,22,27; 5:17) and the expression "humble one's soul" in relation to fasting (Ps 35:13; 69:11).

The Book of Jubilees

Jub 50,12f lists a number of activities, including fasting, which, if done on the sabbath, would make one liable to death. This book was written in Palestine, in Hebrew, perhaps as early as 200–160 B.C., or somewhat later, but certainly before 100 B.C.[5] It emphasizes the need for an exact observance of the sabbath and of the feasts. It was particularly important to the monks of Qumran, although it seems to originate from earlier levitical circles.

The statement forbidding fasting on the sabbath implies that certain groups did want to fast on the sabbath. The Book of Jubilees itself has no special interest in fasting; it often speaks of "eating and drinking before the Lord" (22,5f; 49,6,9) or "eating and drinking" on the sabbath (2,21,31; 50,9).

Fragment of a Zadokite Work

Chapter XIII, 13 of this fragment states: "No man shall fast of his own will on the sabbath." This work was written after the Book of Jubilees but before the destruction of the Temple, that is, between 106 B.C. and 70 A.D., perhaps between 106 B.C. and 57 B.C.[6] Once again, the command not to fast on the sabbath implies that some wanted to do just that.

The Books of Adam and Eve

According to Vita Adae et Evae VI,1, Adam fasted for forty days, and according to the Slavonic version, XXXV,2f, he fasted for

---

4. Eissfeldt, 613; Denis, 64.
5. Eissfeldt, 606–608; Denis, 161f.
6. R.H. Charles, *The Apocrypha and Pseudepigrapha of the Old Testament.* Vol. 2, *Pseudepigrapha* (Oxford: Clarendon Press, 1913) 787.

forty days while Eve fasted for forty-four days, as a penance. This book may have originated in Hebrew between 20 B.C. and 70 A.D., but its date of composition is disputed.[7]

THE PHARISEES

A description of the attitude of the Pharisees toward fasting, as distinct from that of other Jewish groups in the time of Jesus, can be derived only indirectly from the Talmud, with the realization that its halachic prescriptions, meant for the whole populace, stem from the rabbinic stream of thought, itself an outgrowth of Pharisaism in the Second Commonwealth, and that its haggadic figures, examples of pious rabbis, embody Pharisaic ideals.[8] The Talmud is not much concerned with historical progression, and so we run the danger of projecting into the past characteristics of a later period. One reassuring note is the fact that the laws concerning fasting in the Talmud are basically the same as those found in the Old Testament. All the types of fasting encountered in the Old Testament reappear in the Talmud. The central fast continues to be *Yom Kippur;* the four commemorative fast days of Zech 7:3ff and 8:19 are taken up again; special fasts declared in time of drought and other calamities are still popular, and private fasts continue to be practiced.

Ta'anit ("Fasts")

Although there are many parts of the Talmud that treat of fasting, a study of the Book of Fasts, the Babylonian Ta'anit, will be particularly reflective of the mind of the rabbis and, with due caution, of the Pharisees.[9] The Ta'anit consists of four chapters dealing with special fasts decreed for the community because of drought and other forms of divine visitation such as pestilence. Fasting, prayer, and ceremonial acts such as taking the ark to the public square and cloth-

7. Eissfeldt, 637: 20 B.C.-70 A.D.; Denis, 14, gives a short history of the complex question.

8. J. Neusner, *From Politics to Piety. The Emergence of Pharisaic Judaism* (Englewood Cliffs: Prentice-Hall, 1973).

9. A translation of this book is found in The *Babylonian Talmud, Seder Mo'ed,* tr. and ed. by I. Epstein (London: Soncino Press, 1938).

ing oneself in sackcloth and pouring ashes on one's head were meant to awaken the community to a sense of its guilt, to repentance and humiliation before God, and thus to appease his anger.

As a whole, the attitude of the Ta'anit toward fasting is positive. Many of the rabbis' discussions take the idea of fasting for granted, and the points raised usually deal with such specifics as to when or how certain practices are to be carried out.

Prayer is an ever-present companion of fasting. The Ta'anit is careful to teach that fasting is not some kind of magic practice to force rain. Far from it. The need for interior repentance along with fasting is mentioned many times.

Sometimes a fast is "answered" because of the merit of the one fasting. Rabbi fasted, and it did not rain, but after 'Ilfa fasted and prayed it did. Rabbi then asked him, "What is your special merit?" 'Ilfa explained that he took special care to secure wine for Kiddush and Habdalah.[10] Rab fasted, but it did not rain; then the reader prayed, and it rained. Rab asked him, "What is your special merit?" The reader explained that he teaches the children of the poor as well as those of the rich and that he takes no fees from those who cannot afford to pay. Yet just to make sure that no one presume on his own merits, there follows a list of incidences where a rabbi fasted and prayed for rain unsuccessfully, and was then grieved and humiliated, and rain fell.

For continued drought, a first fast of three days, Monday, Thursday, and Monday, is to be observed. If it does not rain, a further fast of three days is to be held, and if this too is ineffective, a final series of seven fast days is to be kept, always on Monday and Thursday. The ritual for the seven fast days is then given, and concludes with a discussion about the Ninivites, which points out that the purpose of the fast is to humble oneself before God, not in order to pressure him, but to beg his mercy. Jon 3:8 is quoted, "Let them cry mightily to God," and the Talmud continues: "What did they say? They said, Master of the Universe, if one is submissive and the other is not, if one is righteous and the other is not, who of them should yield?" Epstein comments: "Man cannot force God to yield

---

10. Babylonian Ta'anit 24a.

to him; God should, however, in his great loving-kindness yield to the prayer of a man who humiliates himself before him."[11]

The Ta'anit also teaches that one should complete one's fast even after the prayer has been answered: "Our rabbis have taught: if one fasted on account of some visitation and it passed, or for a sick person and he got well, he should nevertheless complete his fast."[12] The visitation has passed, but to show that the fast implied more than just a means of making it pass, one was to complete the fast as an act of filial piety to God.

Although the Ta'anit is thus generally in favor of fasting, there are also several texts which deny the value of fasting. They are few in number, but they seem to have exercised great influence.

One text states that the scholar should not fast: Rabbi Shesheth said, "The young scholar who would afflict himself by fasting let a dog devour his meal."[13] Rabbi Jeremiah ben Abba said in the name of Resh Lakish: "A scholar may not afflict himself by fasting because he thereby lessens his heavenly work," that is, he weakens himself by fasting and consequently his studies suffer.[14]

The other text is far more universal in its condemnation of fasting: "Samuel said, 'Whosoever fasts is termed a sinner.' He is of the same opinion as the following Tanna. For it has been taught: Eleazar ha-Kappar Berabbi says, What is Scripture referring to when it says (of the Nazirite) 'And make atonement for him, for that he sinned by reason of the soul.' Against which soul did he sin? He denied himself wine. We can now make this inference from minor to major: if this man who denied himself wine only is termed sinner, how much more so he who denies himself the enjoyment of so many things."[15] The discussion that follows in the Talmud is complicated, for in Num 6:5 the Nazirite is also called holy, so how can he be a sinner? One answer is that he defiled himself. This is not very satisfactory, but no clear counter-statement is offered.

Contemporary articles on fasting usually stress that the rabbis

11. Epstein, *Seder Mo'ed*, 75.
12. Bab. Ta'an. 10b.
13. *Ibid.*, 11b.
14. *Ibid.*
15. *Ibid.*, 11a.

discouraged ascetical fasting, and quote the above statements by Samuel and Rabbi Shesheth as proof. Moshe Herr cites Samuel and comments: "This led to a trend in the halacha which sought to limit even public fasts and their severity, emphasizing however at the same time the original significance of fasting—good deeds and repentance."[16] S. Lowy, after giving examples of rabbis whose "teeth were blackened from fasting," adds: "It would be wrong to assume that an ascetic tendency toward extensive fasting was prevalent. On the whole, Judaism was set against such extreme practices. From the very earliest times—even before the ascetic sects came into existence—down to the amoraic period such practices were generally discouraged."[17]

The statements in the Ta'anit against fasting refer to private fasts. The reason for Samuel's statement is not given, nor for that of Eleazar ha-Kappar, but in view of the importance which these texts later had, they probably reflect the feeling that self-imposed fasts lead to pride and self-esteem, and would lack the safeguards of communal fasting, of humble submission to the loving mercy of God for his people, the whole community. The main tendency of the Talmud texts on fasting is to emphasize community fasts, carried out with prayer and humility. The Talmud also manifests a desire for sanctity as shown in the examples of the great rabbis. The individual is seen as part of the group.

We may conclude that the Pharisees in the time of Jesus probably fasted twice a week as Lk 18:12 and Did 8,1 point out, on Monday and Thursday, but it would be a mistake to universalize the spirit of pride and self-righteousness that is the characteristic of the Pharisee in the Lucan account. Pride may well have been a constant hazard,[18] but the Pharisaic traditions, continued in the Talmud, tried to defuse the danger by emphasizing the need for humility, inner conversion, and confidence that God would hear because of his graciousness. Proper attitudes were taught also by citing the example of

16. M. Herr, "Fasting and Fast Days," *Encyclopaedia Judaica* VI, 1194 (1971).

17. S. Lowy, "The Motivation of Fasting in Talmudic Literature," *JJS* 9 (1958) 22–24.

18. That this is a universal danger has been brilliantly shown by F. Kafka, "A Hunger Artist," *The Complete Stories,* ed. by N. Glatzer (New York: Schocken Books, 1971), 268–277.

the holy rabbis, a process that undoubtedly dates back to biblical times. The message was there for anyone who wished to accept it. The lack of a doctrine about the imprisonment of a spiritual soul in a carnal body kept them from certain ascetical excesses of later groups, for fasting is never mentioned in biblical or rabbinic texts as the means of being released from dependence on a sinful body. Its focal point was not the spiritual superiority of the one who practiced it, but the humbling of self before an omnipotent God.

The Monks of Qumran

There is some debate as to the exact time of the founding of the Qumran community by the Teacher of Righteousness, whether during the reign of Jonathan, high priest from 152–143 B.C., or during the high-priestly term of his successor, Simon, 143–134 B.C., but most indications point to the former as the Wicked Priest from whom the Teacher of Righteousness disassociated himself and who occasioned the settlement at Qumran.[19] The Teacher of Righteousness was a priest, and possibly a high priest, who had irreconcilable differences with the leadership in the Temple, and who therefore led a group of priests and laymen into the desert at Qumran in order to establish a center of true worship there.[20]

The monks of Qumran were convinced that the sacrifices offered in the Temple were invalid,[21] that atonement for sin was not being carried out,[22] and that they were called, in accordance with the eternal will of God, to take its place. They did not offer sacrifices at Qumran,[23] but they did consider their whole way of life as its equivalent and therefore as having the salvific value of atonement for sin.

19. R. de Vaux, *Archaeology and the Dead Sea Scrolls* (London: Oxford University Press, 1973) 127–138.
20. 1QpHab II,8; 4QpPs37 III,15f show he was a priest.
21. CD XX,22; VI,11f; 1QpHab XII,7–9; cf. G. Klinzing, *Die Umdeutung des Kultus in der Qumrangemeinde und im Neuen Testament* (Göttingen: Vandenhoeck & Ruprecht, 1971) 11.
22. Klinzing, 100–102, 151.
23. De Vaux, *Archaeology,* 14; O. Betz, "Le ministère cultuel dans la secte de Qumrân et dans le Christianisme primitif," *La secte de Qumrân et les origines du Christianisme,* Recherches Bibliques IV, ed. by J. van der Ploeg et al. (Desclée de Brouwer, 1959) 163–202.

Theirs was a priestly life, a spiritual priesthood with a spiritual sacrifice of praise and perfect obedience to the Law. Their spiritualization of the Temple sacrifice was not complete, however, and they did envision a return to sacrifices in the sabbatical year during the eschatological battle.[24]

Many elements of their way of life derive from the consciousness of being a priestly community, as if they were in service at the Temple. The washing ritual was considered a source of cultic purification, in order to partake of the sacred meal in a special room, similar to the regulations of Lev 22:6 and Num 18:10f. The meal itself was sacred, as if eaten by priests in the Temple. The discovery at Qumran of over a hundred piles of bones of sheep, goats, and cattle, carefully covered with sherds and either buried in shallow holes or perhaps even left above ground, attests to the special nature of the bones and to the sacred character of the meals at which this meat was eaten.[25]

Even the practice of celibacy on the part of the full members of the community seems to have its roots in the sexual purity of the priest in service at the Temple, although the consciousness of being the people of the New Covenant about to encounter the Lord on Mount Sinai, with abstention from sex as a requirement of purity (Ex 19:15), also played a part.[26]

Their poverty and the need to hand over all goods to the community, under the care of a guardian, a *mbqr,* stems from a concern for ritual purity, not to be contaminated, but it also reflects the uni-

---

24. 1QM II, 5–6; J. Carmignac, *La régle de la guerre* (Paris: Letouzey et Ané, 1958) xv and 30f.

25. De Vaux, *Archaeology,* 12f.

26. O. Betz, "The Eschatological Interpretation of the Sinai-Tradition in Qumran and in the New Testament," *RQ* 6(1967–68) 90f. Celibacy at Qumran certainly existed, but its extent is questioned. Philo states they were celibate, *Hypothetica* 11,14–17; Josephus writes that they "neglect wedlock, but choose out other persons' children, while they are pliable" (*Wars* II,8,2), but then treats of a second group (*Wars* II,8,13) who live like the others, except in the matter of marriage. The Manual of Discipline (1QS) presupposes a group of unmarried men, whereas CD, 1QM, and 1QSa mention also women and children. Cf. de Vaux, *Archaeology,* 115,128f on the finds in the cemetery. All indications point to the fact that one group was celibate, probably the fully initiated, and the other was married.

fied management of property among the Temple priests and levites.[27] Their dedication to the study of the Law and their call to "distinguish between clean and unclean" and to "proclaim the difference between holy and profane" (CD VI,17–18) are all priestly duties (Lev 10:10; Ez 44:23).

Fasting

Surprisingly, in view of the strenuous life full of renunciation led at Qumran, fasting is hardly ever mentioned. In the texts found so far, there are only three explicit references to fasting, and all center on the Day of Atonement (Damascus Document CD VI,18–20; Pesher Habakkuk IQpHab XI,4–8; and Temple Scroll TS XXV,10—XXVII,10). Although a strict fast is presumed on that day as in the rest of Israel, the primary concern here is the date. The monks of Qumran clearly followed a calendar different from that of the Temple priests, and this was a major bone of contention between the two groups.[28] J.T. Milik goes so far as to say that "the calendar question, as we see from the Qumran writings, provides a thoroughly satisfactory reason for the Essene schism."[29]

A more fruitful avenue towards an understanding of the Qumran attitude on fasting is provided by the pesher on Psalm 37 4QpPs37 II,8–10 and III,2b–5:[30]

"The meek shall possess the land, and delight themselves in abundant prosperity" (Ps 37:11). Its interpretation concerns the congregation of the poor who accept the *period of affliction* and are saved from all the traps of Belial. Afterwards all those who have taken possession of the earth

27. A. Steiner, "Warum lebten die Essener asketisch?" *BZ* 15(1971) 1–28, esp. 18.

28. A. Jaubert, *The Date of the Last Supper* (Staten Island: Alba, 1965).

29. J.T. Milik, *Ten Years of Discovery in the Wilderness of Judaea* (London: SCM Press, 1959) 111.

30. D. Pardee, "A Restudy of the Commentary on Psalm 37 from Qumran Cave 4," *RQ* 8 (1973/74) 167.

shall delight and grow fat on all the (...) of the flesh (II,8–10).

"In the time of hunger they shall be satisfied, for the evil ones shall perish" (Ps 37:19b,20a). Its interpretation is (that) he will revive them in famine, in the *period of affliction* when many will perish by famine and pestilence, that is, all who did not go (out from there) to be wi(th) the congregation of his chosen ones (III,2b–5).

The key phrase in both these passages is *mw'd ht'nyt,* "period of affliction." It can be translated in two different ways, either "time of the fast" or "season of affliction." In the first instance it would mean that future prosperity is promised to the monks of Qumran, the "congregation of the poor," because they "accept the time of the fast," the Qumran date for the celebration of the Day of Atonement. According to the second translation, "season of affliction," it would refer to the present time as a period of stress which will be followed in the eschatological future by a period of joy. There are problems of translation in either case, but both are possible, and indeed both are supported by "incontrovertible arguments."[31] Most probably both meanings are intended, as a "double entendre," in a deliberate allusion to Ezr 9:5, the only place in the Hebrew Bible where the noun *t'nyt* appears, which can be translated as "fasting" (RSV) and which became the technical term for fasting in the Talmud, but which the older translations rendered as "affliction" or "humiliation" (LXX: *tapeinōsis;* Vg:*adflictio;*—modern translations too: NAB, NEB, JB), and which gave rise to a discussion about the meaning of the text in the Talmud.[32] The "period of affliction," *mw'd t'nyt,* is then the present pain of suffering and persecution accepted by the monks of Qumran, occasioned by their acceptance of a different time for the fast of the Day of Atonement, but which will be rewarded by the joys of a messianic banquet.

Barbara Thiering's articles on the suffering and asceticism at

31. R.B. Coote, "MW'D HT'NYT in 4Q 171 (Pesher Psalm 37), fragments 1–2, col. II, line 9," *RQ* 8 (1972/75) 81–85.

32. *Ibid.,* 83.

Qumran emphasize especially the monks' eschatological intensity.[33]
By their striving for a superhuman mode of existence they wanted to
bring on the age of eschatological justice when all evil would be de-
stroyed, even though they knew that the final age would come when
it was supposed to come by God's unalterable plan. Like a woman
about to give birth, they suffered the birth pangs of bringing the eschaton into existence, even though, like the birth of a child, there
was no stopping it. A. Steiner also allows for the eschatological dimension of the monks' thinking, even though he would emphasize
first and foremost their concept of being a new, spiritual priesthood,
called to effect atonement by the spiritual sacrifice of their holiness
of life, since the bloody sacrifice offered in the Temple by an unworthy high priest was invalid.[34] Both are important: their awareness
that they are the substitute for worship in the Temple, and their consciousness of preparing for the end time.

A final expression used at Qumran deserves comment in the
context of fasting, even though it cannot be shown to refer to fasting
in Qumran, though it does in the Old Testament and the Talmud:
'nh npš, to "humble oneself," 1QS III,8:

> He will be cleansed from all his iniquities; and in an up-
> right and humble spirit his sin will be atoned, and in the
> submission of his soul (wb'nwt npšw) to all the statutes of
> God his flesh will be cleansed. . . .

There was a great emphasis in Qumran on humility before God. It
would not be stretching the point too far by seeing in this concept an
important insight into the Qumran attitude toward fasting, along
with other aspects of their spirituality: humble intensity before the
Lord and his spirit at the coming of the eschaton.

R. de Vaux, the main excavator of the Qumran ruins, drew attention to the extreme poverty of the area. It was barely possible to
live there. This certainly affected their diet. We conclude then that

---

33. B. Thiering, "The Biblical Source of Qumran Asceticism," *JBL* 93 (1974)
429–444; *idem,* "Suffering and Asceticism at Qumran, as Illustrated in the Hodayot,"
RQ 8 (1972/75) 393–405.

34. Steiner, "Warum lebten die Essener asketisch?" 6–9.

the monks of Qumran did not have any major interest in fasting as such, except for absolute fidelity to the accuracy of the time for celebrating the Day of Atonement, but they lived and ate very poorly, and accepted their time of affliction humbly, in an intense expectation that a glorious end would soon come.

JOSEPHUS

Josephus (37/38-c.101 A.D.) mentions fasting on occasion in his works. He speaks of the Day of Atonement as "the Fast" (*Ant* XVIII,94) or as "the day when all observe the fast in honor of God" (*Wars* V,236), and briefly explains the rites observed: ". . . they fast until evening and sacrifice a bull, two rams, seven lambs and a kid as a sin-offering" (*Ant* III,240). In dating events he notices that Jerusalem was taken by the Romans (63 B.C.) "on the fast day" (*Ant* XIV,66), and by the troops of Herod and Sossius twenty-seven years later, on exactly the same day, "the feast of fasting" (*Ant* XIV,487).

Josephus refers to the fast of Ezra and companions before their return from Babylon (as in Ezr 8:21–23), "in order to offer prayers to God for their safety . . . on the journey," and points out that God heard their prayer (*Ant* XI,134). He describes with flourish the fast of King Izates who was threatened by the Parthians: ". . . he gave himself to supplicating God's favor. He flung himself on the ground and befouled his head with ashes; he fasted, together with his wife and children, calling upon God . . . Thus he cried aloud with tears and lamentation, and God hearkened to him" (*Ant* XX,89–91). In his work against Apion, Josephus points out with pride that many nations have taken over Jewish beliefs and pious practices, including the fasts (*Ap* II,282).

Josephus is an important witness to the Jewish institution of fasting and to its spirit of penance for sin and supplication for deliverance.

CHAPTER THREE

Fasting in the Hellenistic World

In the last chapter we saw briefly various expressions of fasting where the predominant influence was the Old Testament—the Apocrypha, the Ta'anit (Book of Fasts) of the rabbis; the Dead Sea Scrolls of Qumran, and the historical works of Josephus. The ideas on fasting in the New Testament relate to this culture, though the mission and person of Jesus will make a significant difference. Before entering into a study of the New Testament, it might be well to see what the Greeks thought about fasting, and how Greek ideals influenced the writings of Philo and the practices of that extraordinary group of men and women near Alexandria, the Therapeutai. This should provide an interesting contrast to the world of the Bible.

FASTING AMONG THE GREEKS[1]

With the exception of oracular shrines, fasting played only a small part in the worship of ancient Greece. It is mentioned only in relation to the cult of Demeter, in whose honor the three-day Attic Thesmophoria were held; the second day was a day of fast. In general, priests were not required to fast before performing an act of worship, and still less the people. Later, through Oriental influence, fasting and food observances became common, especially in the mys-

---

1. R. Arbesmann, "Fasting and Prophecy in Pagan and Christian Antiquity," *Traditio* 7 (1949/51) 1–72; *idem*, art. "Fasten," *Reallexikon für Antike und Christentum* VII, 447–493 (1969); L. Ziehen, art. "Nēsteia," Pauly-Wissowa, XVII,1, 88–107 (1936).

tery religions such as Kybele, which demanded by way of initiation a seven-day avoidance of many kinds of vegetables, apples, pomegranates, dates, fish, pork, and wine, culminating in a full day of fasting. The initiation rites of the Eleusian mysteries also prescribed fasting along with abstinence from many kinds of food.

Often those who gave oracles had to fast. It was felt that demonic forces inhabited certain foods, and those who wished to come into contact with the divine had to be in the state of ritual purity. The prophet of Claros had to abstain from all food for a whole day and night before drinking the spring water which was filled with mantic power and which allowed him to utter the oracle; a similar rite was performed by the prophetess of Didyma, and probably also by the prophets and priestesses of Delphi, Patara, and Delos.

Related to the fasts of the personnel at oracular shrines was the practice of *incubatio,* sleeping in the temples of certain deities in order to obtain prophetic dreams. According to Philostratus, a person consulting the oracle of Amphiaraüs at Oropus in Attica had to fast completely for one day and abstain from wine for three.[2]

Dreams were considered a way of contacting the gods and of receiving divine guidance, but many kinds of food, especially beans, were thought to produce confused dreams and therefore had to be avoided. Galen and other medical authorities held that a low diet produced clear dreams. Apollonius of Tyana ate only bread, dried fruits, and vegetables, preferring wild herbs to garden-grown varieties, in order to keep his senses clear and to discern what would happen in the future.

The vegetarian diet of the Pythagoreans followed this same line of thought. Iamblichus, in his *De vita pythagorica,* states: "Whatever was an obstacle to mantic activity (and to association with the gods), or to the clearness and purity of the soul, or to the state of moderation and virtue, this he recommended avoiding."[3]

Common to these instances of purification by abstaining from certain dishes, especially those causing flatulence, or by fasting completely, is the thought that the soul could reach its greatest power when it was independent of the digestive activity of the body and of

---

2. *Vit. Apoll.* II,37, text cited by Ziehen, "Nēsteia," 93.
3. Lines 106f, cited by Arbesmann, "Fasting and Prophecy," 28.

the evil spirits that inhabit certain foods, so that it could then enter into free communion with the divine world and learn its mysteries through oracles and dreams.

A somewhat different concern can be recognized in the thought of certain philosophical sects such as the Cynics and the Stoics. The Cynics strove toward *enkrateia,* self-control, and wanted to remove everything from their life that was not absolutely necessary. They ate as little as possible, and limited themselves to simple vegetarian foods: bread, hyssop, beans, figs, various fruits and herbs; their drink was water. The Stoics wished to arrive at inner freedom and happiness, *eudaimonia,* through the right use of reason. Their attempt to overcome all emotions which hinder a reasoned approach to human existence led them to adopt a very simple diet, only enough to sustain life. Fundamentally, this was also the ideal of the Epicurean peace of soul.

We see in the Greek world, then, a feeling that the evil spirits which inhabit certain foods hinder the communication of the soul with the world of the gods and its consequent knowledge of the future through dreams. At the same time, various rational philosophic movements aimed at attaining inner peace through self-control. This is in rather stark contrast to the Jewish emphasis on humility, penance, and supplication before Yahweh, the living God.

PHILO

We know only one exact date in the life of Philo—his trip to Rome at the head of a delegation of Jewish citizens of Alexandria in the winter of 39/40 A.D. to see Caesar Gaius Caligula. From this, and some indirect evidence, it seems that he was born about 20 B.C. and died about 45 A.D. His brother Alexander was the financial backer of Herod Agrippa I, and Philo too possessed great wealth, which was probably inherited. He was much involved in politics, but functioned at the same time as a sort of spiritual guide to the Jews of Alexandria.

Much of his teaching about fasting is related to explanations of the Day of Atonement. In *Legatio ad Caium,* 306, he states that the high priest enters the Holy of Holies only once a year, on the "Fast," in order to burn incense there and to pray "according to tradition for abundance of goods, prosperity, and peace for all men." Fasting is here connected with prayer of petition for material blessings and for world peace. In *De posteritate Caini,* 48, he emphasizes the need for humility in order to pray for the remission of sins: "It is commanded on the 10th day of the month to humble one's soul, that is, to put away pride; this setting aside effects a supplication of pardon for voluntary and involuntary sins." We are still primarily in the area of Hebrew thought.

Philo shows Greek influence especially when he contrasts fasting with feasting by a paradox: those who feast are empty and famished (spiritually), whereas those who fast enjoy the satiety of sobriety! In *De ebrietate,* 147–148, he points out that sober men like Samuel are "inebriated" by their possession of God, while those who are drunk with wine pass their whole life without tasting wisdom, and so are always famished because of their continuous "fast"! In *De migratione Abrahami,* 204, he notes that "thought" suffers famine in the midst of the feasting of the senses, but that it experiences joy in the midst of fasting. The Greek ideal of self-control is here evident, as well as the concentration on the individual.

The delicate integration of Hebrew and Greek thought about fasting can be seen in Philo's explanation of the Day of Atonement in *De specialibus legibus* II, 193–203. He contrasts the Atonement with sumptuous feasts and notes that "the very wise Moses" actually named the fast a "feast," and indeed the greatest of feasts, for three reasons: first, because it teaches self-control; second, because the whole day is taken up with prayer; and third, because of the season, the annual harvest, that is, instead of immediately eating their produce like gluttons, the Jews fast in order to teach their spirit not to be proud of their harvest, but to say a prayer of thanksgiving to the heavenly Father "who can nourish and maintain life either with the aid of these things, or even without, as in the desert."

A final tribute to fasting is found in *De migratione Abrahami,* 98, which states that fasting is an offering and, together with perseverance, "the most worthy and most perfect of offerings."

Philo was a great propagandist of virtue and of the religious value of Jewish customs. In the matter of fasting he represented well the significance of the Jewish practice, and explained carefully the motifs

of Yom Kippur—reconciliation with God, forgiveness of sins, petition of blessings, thanksgiving, and humility. To these Jewish themes
he skillfully added the Greek ideal of perfection and *enkrateia,* self-
control.

THE THERAPEUTAI

The Therapeutai are a fascinating group of men and women
who were friends of Philo and who lived an extraordinary life of contemplation and fasting.

Our only explicit source of information about them is Philo's *De
vita contemplativa,*[4] which contrasts their life of contemplation with
the active life of the Essenes. Eusebius thought that Philo was really
describing Christians, and later even the authenticity of *De vita contemplativa* was questioned, but toward the end of the nineteenth century the authorship of Philo was clearly established through the
efforts of Renan, Massebieau, and Conybeare. The discoveries at
Qumran have removed many of the objections against the historicity
of the Therapeutai, and today the real existence of this extraordinary
group of men and women on the shore of Lake Mareotis near Alexandria is generally acknowledged.[5] It has also become increasingly
clear that Philo himself joined the Therapeutai community from
time to time.[6] It was a Jewish sect in northern Egypt, and was quite
open to the Hellenistic culture, as is seen by the fact that women too
were allowed to be members on an equal basis. Still, we must be cau-
tious in our use of Philo's treatise, for he wrote it as an apologia for
the life of contemplation and did not hesitate to idealize his charac-

4. P. Geoltrain, "Le traité de la vie contemplative de Philon d'Alexandrie. Introduction, traduction, et notes," *Semitica* 10 (1960) 5–67; see also the edition of *De
vita contemplativa* in the series *Les Oeuvres de Philon d'Alexandrie,* Vol. 29 (Paris: Du
Cerf, 1963), with notes by F. Daumas.

5. Geoltrain, "Le traité de la vie contemplative," 26; F. Daumas, "La 'Soli-
tude' des Thérapeutes et les antécedents égytpiens du monachisme chrétien," *Philon
d'Alexandrie,* Actes du Colloque National du Centre National de la Recherche Scien-
tifique, Lyon, 11–15 Septembre 1966 (Paris, 1967) 347–359, where the author concen-
trates on the geographical accuracy of Philo's account as an indication of historicity.

6. *Legum allegoriae* II, 85; *De specialibus legibus* III, 1ff; *De Abrahamo* 22–23;
Geoltrain, 26.

ters or to present them according to the categories of Stoic philosophy, which might not have been the way the Therapeutai themselves interpreted their goals. We are on surer ground in accepting the concrete details about their life, though these too are often incomplete.

The Therapeutai gave all their possessions to relatives or friends (*De vit. cont.* 13-18), lived a celibate life,[7] each one alone in a simple house, in a sort of sectarian village, with the houses separated from each other but not too far. They prayed twice a day, in the morning and in the evening, and spent most of the rest of their time alone in a sacred room (*monastērion*) meditating on the Scriptures, on the allegorical writings of the founders of their sect (29), and composed chants and hymns. They neither ate nor drank during the day (34), but consumed a light meal only after sundown.

They lived alone for six days (30) and gathered together every seventh day in a common room where the men and women were separated from each other by a barrier which went from the floor almost to the ceiling but not quite, so that the women too could hear the speaker (32–33). Each one sat in strict order of age.

On the fiftieth day they held a "sacred banquet" in common (71). They came together in the evening, dressed in white. They reclined around the tables, the men on the right and the women on the left—the separating wall had apparently been removed—and they listened in silence to the leader's allegorical explanation of Sacred Scripture. At the end they applauded and chanted hymns.

They then ate their sacred meal: leavened bread, salt mixed with hyssop, and clear water (73 and 81). Afterward they formed two choirs, one of men and one of women, chanted hymns to God, clapped their hands and danced rhythmically to the chant. They then came together to form only one choir and spent the whole night singing together. In the morning, at sunrise, they all turned toward the east and with hands raised up to heaven prayed for a happy day. After the prayer each one retired to his or her house (83–89).

---

7. *De vit. cont.* 18;68; Daumas, notes to *De vit. cont.*, 127–129; V. Nikiprowetzky, "Les suppliants chez Philon d'Alexandrie," *Revue des études juives* 122 (1963) 241–278, esp. 265–270 and 276f.

Food

Some of the Therapeutai fasted completely for three days, and others even for six; no one ate or drank during the day (34f). We have already seen how simply they ate at the sacred banquet on the fiftieth day. In paragraph 37 of *De vita contemplativa* Philo tells us what they ate the rest of the time—ordinary bread, salt, hyssop, and spring water—but it is not clear whether he is talking about every day or simply the sabbath. Since the preceding paragraphs 30 to 33 and 36 (but not 34 and 35) deal with the sabbath observance, it is likely that he is simply referring to the menu for the sabbath. Such a meal needed no immediate preparation and was well suited to the perfect keeping of the sabbath. But it is also possible, and even probable, that bread, salt, hyssop, and water constituted the bulk of their daily diet. Ordinary bread was the basic food of the poor in antiquity.[8] It is the minimum necessary for subsistence. Given the Therapeutai's desire for contemplation and almost complete neglect of physical activity, it may well be that they were satisfied with the absolute minimum. On the other hand it is also possible that Philo simply idealized his heroes and wanted to imply that they ate every day as little as they did on the sabbath. He never says, for instance, that they drank wine, and yet in his description of their fiftieth-day banquet he explains: "Wine is not served on those days" and "The table is free of any food in which there is blood" (73). It would seem then that the Therapeutai were allowed to drink wine on other days. Whether that is also true of meat is another question. The text about unbloody food does not imply that on other days meat was served. The Therapeutai were probably vegetarians like the Pythagoreans.[9] But the sentence, "The table is free of any food in which there is blood" (par. 73), could also be an allusion to Lev 17:10–14, which forbids the eating of blood, but which does not forbid the eating of

8. Daumas, 105, note on *De vit. cont.* 37; J. Carcopino, *La vie quotidienne à Rome a l'apogée de l'empire* (Paris: Hachette, 1948) 305.

9. Daumas, 134f, note on *De vit. cont.* 73; Geoltrain, "Le traité de la vie contemplative," 27; there are many points of contact with the Pythagoreans, including reverence for the number 50, "the number of purity and of perpetual virginity" (*De vit. cont.* 65), and celibacy.

meat which had been drained of blood. In any case, Philo never says that the Therapeutai ate meat.

The underlying motivation which prompted the Therapeutai to live such a rigid and ascetic life was probably quite complex. They were Jewish sectarians, and many of their practices seem like a spiritualization of priestly worship in the Temple, much like the monks of Qumran: the wearing of a white linen garment (38;66; Ex 28:40–43; Ez 44:17) for their sacred meal at which there was no wine (73; Lev 10:9); Philo himself says that they ate their bread leavened and their salt mixed with hyssop out of respect for the unleavened bread and pure salt in the Temple (81f; Lev 24:5–9), which means that they considered their sacred meal as a reduced celebration of the cult in the Temple;[10] their celibacy (18;68; Ex 19:15,22–25; Lev 15:18; 22:4; 1 Sam 21:4f), and even their poverty (13; Ez 44:28).

Yet there is no evidence that the Therapeutai, like the monks of Qumran, would have considered themselves called to replace an invalid worship in the Temple; their primary scope seems to have been the worship of God through pure contemplation. Their quiet way of renunciation was conducted in the service of wisdom and knowledge of God. There were no scourgings or beatings of the body, but they did want to purify their inner being. Philo does not even use the verb *nēsteuein* in describing their fasts; he says they "forgot" to eat, so full were they of the joy of wisdom (35). Their life was an example of the *sobria ebrietas* so dear to Philo. Elsewhere (34) he points out that the basis of all their other virtues was *enkrateia*, "self-control," a concept which has a history dating back to Plato and which was especially emphasized by the Stoics and by Philo himself. They were also concerned about humility and equality; they had no slaves, and even the young members who served at table on the day of the banquet wore their tunic long, in order to show that there was nothing servile about them (39; 69–72). We see in the Therapeutai, then, motifs which derive from both Jewish and Hellenistic sources, with contemplation of God as the main goal.

---

10. Geoltrain, 20: M. Delcor, "Repas cultuels esséniens et thérapeutes. Thiases et haburoth," *RQ* (1967/69) 409f.

CHAPTER FOUR

Fasting in the Desert
(Mt 4:1-4/Lk 4:1-4)

The scene of Jesus fasting forty days in the desert made a great impression on the early Church. Tertullian pointed out that Jesus fasted for forty days after his baptism, and wondered whether or not the Christians too should follow his example and fast after their baptism. After stating the objection that perhaps they should not, for the newly baptized were rather to rejoice with gratitude for having received salvation, he nevertheless concluded that they should fast, for fasting drives out the temptations which come through a full and immoderate stomach.[1] In *De jejunio* he said that there was no better way of understanding Christ than by fasting often.[2] Irenaeus wrote that Jesus fasted forty days after the example of Moses and Elijah and was hungry, in order to demonstrate his true humanity and to give the devil an area where he could attack. Unlike Adam who, though he was not hungry, transgressed by eating, Jesus, who was hungry, did not allow the devil to dissuade him from waiting for the nourishment which comes from God.[3] Ambrose taught that Jesus prescribed forty days of fasting for all Christians. Ephraem, Hilary of Poitiers, Augustine, and Leo the Great also pointed to the forty days' fast of Jesus as an example for us.

Given the complex state of contemporary exegesis, one would hardly expect to make such immediate applications today as did the early Church Fathers. And yet can we simply dismiss the biblical ac-

---

1. *De baptismo* 20; CSEL XX,217.
2. CSEL, XX,283.
3. *Adv. haer.* V,21,2.

count as myth and therefore as no longer relevant to the twentieth century? There is a *via media,* a way of determining the meaning of the scriptural text, and, once that has been accurately accomplished, of applying it to our own situation.

The passages on fasting in the desert must be considered from a threefold point of view: at the level of redaction, previous oral and written tradition, and in terms of the historical Jesus. We shall analyze the middle level first, that of the traditions behind the Gospels, and then proceed to see how they have been utilized by Mt and Lk in their respective redactions, and, finally, how they relate to the life of Jesus.

The Tradition Behind the Gospels

The temptation of Jesus in the desert is portrayed in Mk 1:12f and in Mt 4:1–4/Lk 4:1–4. The Marcan text does not speak of fasting, so our attention will be directed primarily to the accounts in Mt and Lk.

Both Mt and Lk present three temptations, but the second and third are given in inverse order: Mt ends with Jesus tempted on a high mountain, seemingly a preparation for his final scene, 28:16–20, while Lk ends with the temptation at the pinnacle of the Temple, in accordance with his own theological emphasis on Jerusalem. Opinion among exegetes as to which was the original order of the underlying common text (*Quelle:* "Source") is divided, but most accept it as being that of Mt. This is convincing, for it gives the chronological order of the temptations of Israel as portrayed in the Old Testament: hunger (Ex 16:4), "thou shalt not tempt" (Ex 17:1–7), and worship of idols (Ex 32:1–6). The view of Dibelius, that the three temptation scenes were at one time handed on separately, has not been generally followed.

Attempts have been made to reconstruct the text of Q behind Mt 4:1–4/Lk 4:1–4, but for our purposes it is sufficient to note that the following elements are common to both Mt and Lk:

- Jesus is led in/into the desert by the Spirit;
- he is tempted by the devil;
- he remains forty days;

- he does not eat during this period;
- afterward he is hungry;
- the devil commands him to turn "these stones" (Mt) or "this stone" (Lk) into bread "if you are the Son of God";
- Jesus answers with LXX Dt 8:3, "Man shall not live by bread alone" (Mt adds more).

LITERARY GENRE

In 1914 A. Meyer compared the temptation account to a Jewish haggada and considered it the product of Jewish-Christian erudition, an edifying meditation on Dt 6—8. He said that a Judeo-Christian scribe, starting with Mk 1:12f, a short poetic and mythic presentation of an experience by Jesus, constructed a haggada in which the teaching of Dt about Israel was used to present Jesus as the prototype of those who remain faithful to God in the course of temptation. R. Bultmann agrees, for the dialogue between Jesus and the devil reflects rabbinic disputations, such as the one in Sifre Deut 307, in three parts, with the answer given each time in the form of a citation from Scripture, or the Palestinian Shekalim 5,49b,2 where a rabbi disputes with the lord of the demons and answers him with Scripture.[4] Along these same lines S. Schulz speaks of a "debate based on typically rabbinic models" created by a Hellenistic Judeo-Christian scribe, and B. Gerhardsson names it a "haggadic midrash."[5]

Although there is generally a greater concern among Catholic authors to insist on the basic historicity of the temptation account in the life of Jesus, at least as an inner experience that he would have told his disciples, there is a growing tendency to accept the literary form of this passage as a haggada.[6]

---

4. R. Bultmann, *The History of the Synoptic Tradition*[2] (Oxford: Blackwell, 1972) 254, where he also cites A. Meyer's article. Cf. H. A. Kelly, "The Devil in the Desert," *CBQ* 26 (1964) 190–220.

5. S. Schulz, *Q. Die Spruchquelle der Evangelisten* (Zürich: Theologischer Verlag, 1972) 185; B. Gerhardsson, *The Testing of God's Son (Matt 4:1–11 & Par)* chs.1–4 (Lund: Gleerup, 1966) 7ff.

6. B. Rigaux, *Témoignage de l'évangile de Luc* (Desclée de Brouwer, 1970) 147; X. Léon-Dufour, *L'évangile selon saint Matthieu* (Lyon: Faculté de théologie de Fourvière-Lyon, 1972) 52; H. Schürmann, *Das Lukasevangelium* (Freiburg: Herder, 1969) 220, n. 254.

The arguments presented in favor of this opinion are indeed overwhelming. They could be summed up as follows: (a) the parallels in rabbinic literature; (b) the many references to Moses and the Israelites in the desert, especially as found in Dt 6–8; (c) the obviously symbolic nature of so many elements of the account: the number forty, the "very high mountain," the appearance of the devil, the transpositions from one place of temptation to another, the vision of all the kingdoms of the world; (d) the use of Ps 91 by the devil; (e) the exclusive use of quotes from Dt 6—8 in the answer of Jesus; secondarily, also the fact that Jesus quotes the LXX version, which would point rather to the reverse, namely that someone meditated on the LXX Dt and saw in it a beautiful hidden reference to Jesus; (f) the private nature of the temptations: none of the disciples were there; it precedes the public life of Jesus; (g) the title "Son of God" used in the first two temptations; this too points to the reverse, namely to a meditation on the meaning of that title.

ANALYSIS

From the devil's opening words we know that Jesus is being presented as the "Son of God." This suggests those passages from the Old Testament which connect the ideas of desert, forty, temptation, Spirit, and Son of God. Those most applicable refer to Israel. If we substitute "Lord your God" for "Spirit," then *all* of these themes are present in Dt 8:2–5: "And you shall remember all the ways in which the *Lord your God* has *led* you these *forty* years in the *desert,* that he might humble you, *testing* you. . . . As a man disciplines his *son,* the Lord your God disciplines you." Ex 4:22f also contains the fundamental idea of Israel as son, going into the desert: "You shall say to Pharaoh, Thus says the Lord, Israel is my first-born *son,* and I say to you, let my *son* go that he may serve me." The themes of Spirit and desert with the Israelites are found also in Nm 11:16–30; Is 63:8–14; and Neh 9:19–21. A consideration of the individual images leads to the same conclusion.

1. *Israel as Son of God*[7]

Israel experienced its divine sonship in the events of the Exodus whereby it was formed as a people of God. In Ex 4:22 Yahweh refers to Israel as "my first-born son" who is to be released from Pharaoh's power. Hos 11:1 looks back nostalgically at the formation period of Israel when it was a child, loved by God, who could say of it, "Out of Egypt I called my son." Dt 1:31 reminds the Israelites of the time when "in the wilderness you saw how the Lord God bore you, as a man bears his son." We have already noted the text of Dt 8:5; cf also 14:1. Israel's sonship is emphasized particularly in Dt 32. Jer 3:19 continues this idea, as does Wis 18:13: "They acknowledge thy people to be God's son."

In the Old Testament the king too was considered to be God's son, especially in 2 Sam 7:14; Pss 2:7 and 89:26f. This led to the development of messianism, as in Is 9:5, and probably accounts for the messianic overtones in the temptation scenes. In the first temptation, however, the main focus is on Jesus as a new representative of Israel, undoing by his obedience the sins committed by the ancients in the desert.

2. *Temptation of the Israelites in the Desert*

The word *nissah* (LXX *peirazō*) is used thirty-five times in the Old Testament. Besides the five times when it simply means to "attempt" or "venture", and the six times it is used in a secular context, it appears thirteen times with God as subject, testing men (Abraham, one time; Levi, one time; Hezekiah, one time; the faithful of Ps 26:2, one time; the Israelites, nine times), and eleven times with men as subject, testing God (Gideon, one time; Ahaz, one time; the Israelites, nine times). There are no early references to "temptation" by the devil. Those whom God "tempts," or better, "tests," are not the heathen, but rather his own people, those with whom he has made a covenant. Conversely, those who "test" him are always his own, the

---

7. Much of what follows is indebted to the thorough analysis of these themes by B. Gerhardsson, *The Testing of God's Son,* 20ff.

people he has chosen, the Israelites as a whole, or certain ones such as Gideon and Ahaz. The word is therefore used primarily in a covenant context, and seems to imply a "testing" of the partner to see if he is faithful.

Of the nine times when God is said to test the Israelites, three refer to the time of the Judges (Jgs 2:22; 3:1,4), one to false prophets (Dt 13:4), and the rest to the desert (Ex 15:25; 16:4; 20:20; Dt 8:2,16). With the Israelites as subject, testing God, it is used nine times, once with reference to Palestine (Ps 78:56), and all the other times with reference to the desert (Ex 17:2,7; Nm 14:22; Dt 6:16; Ps 78:17, 41; 95:9; 106:14). Thus the majority of the instances when *nissah* is used in a religious context, it refers to the desert, to the covenant relationship between Israel and Yahweh.

God tested Israel in the desert with his Law (Ex 15:25), with his overpowering appearance on Mount Sinai (Ex 20:20), and by all the things that happened in the desert, especially by their hunger and his feeding them with manna (Ex 16:4; Dt 8:2,16). His motive was a twofold one, to find out whether or not they would be faithful: "whether they will walk in my law or not" (Ex 16:4), "to know what was in your heart, whether you would keep his commandments or not" (Dt 8:2), and also to discipline them: "as a man disciplines his son" (Dt 8:5), "that the fear of him may be before your eyes, that you may not sin" (Ex 20:20), "to do you good in the end" (Dt 8:16).

When the Israelites "tested" God, they showed their lack of faith and trust in him, and thus committed a great sin. Their whole sinfulness in the desert, which later became a standard motif of their comportment at this time, was summed up in the word "temptation": they dared tempt God! According to Ex 17:2 they were thirsty, had no water to drink, and quarreled with Moses, who retorted, "Why do you put the Lord to a test?"—the meaning of which is explained in v.7: "They tested the Lord, saying, 'Is the Lord in our midst or not?' " They should have trusted in his abiding presence and his guidance. That lack of trust was the sin of "tempting" God, so much so that Moses in Ex 17:7 named the place where it occurred "Massah," which is derived from the verb *nissah,* and is called *Peirasmos,* "Temptation," in the LXX! Dt 6:16, from which Jesus quotes in the second temptation, refers explicitly to the sin of Massah: "You shall not put the Lord your God to the test, as you tested him at Massah"; so does Ps 95:9.

Their sin was particularly grievous, for they should have known better, they should have remembered the works Yahweh had performed for them in the past. Nm 14:22 speaks of those "who have seen my glory, and my signs which I wrought in Egypt and the wilderness, and yet have tested me these ten times"; Ps 78:11: "they forgot what he had done, and the miracles he had shown them," and in vv. 41f: "They tested him again and again . . . they did not keep in mind his power"; Ps 106:13f: "But they soon forgot his works . . . they had a wanton craving in the wilderness, and put God to the test in the desert." This last citation brings up a point which we shall discuss more fully in treating the nature of the first temptation of Jesus in the desert: his hunger, reminiscent of the "craving in the wilderness" which led the people to put God to the test.

3. Temptation by Satan

In the older texts, Yahweh himself "tempted," or, better, "tested" the Israelites and certain other chosen pious men such as Abraham or King Hezekiah. In later post-exilic writing there was a tendency to avoid ascribing temptation directly to him, even though it was not denied. Often the passive was used (as in Dan 12:10; Jubil 19,8), or the expression *en peirasmō,* "in temptation" (1 Mac 2:52; Sir 44:20; Test Jos 2,7). In a number of instances the figure of Satan was introduced. In 2 Sam 24:1 it was Yahweh who "incited" David to sin (v.10) by taking a census of the people; in the later version of 1 Chr 21:1 it was *sāṭān.* In Wis 2:24 it was no longer the serpent, one of the wild creatures "that the Lord God has made" (Gen 3:1), who brought about the Fall by his temptation, but rather *diabolos.*

The Book of Job was probably instrumental in this change of emphasis. It is a profound study on the "testing" of the just man through tribulation. According to Jb 42:7 it was Yahweh himself who "inflicted all the evil" on Job, though it was Satan, one "among the sons of God" (1:6), who had been given limited power to harm Job in order to see if he would be faithful in adversity. This process continued and became dominant during the inter-testamental period.

4. Forty Days in the Desert

The fundamental point of view presented so far has been the special relationship of the first temptation of Jesus to that of the people Israel; the argument is based primarily on the many points of contact between Dt 8:2–5 and Mt 4:1–4/Lk 4:1–4. The number forty is one such item. One may ask: Is there really a correspondence between the "forty years" of the Israelites in the desert and the "forty days (and nights)" of Jesus in the desert? Is it proper to equate forty *years* with forty *days?* I believe the answer is yes, for two reasons: first, such a relationship is actually made in the Old Testament, and, second, there is a proportion between forty years in the life of a people and forty days in the life of an individual. Ezekiel had to lie on his right side forty days as a penance for the forty years during which Judah sinned: ". . . to bear the punishment of the house of Judah; *forty days* I assign you, *a day for each year*" (Ez 4:6). A similar principle is applied in Nm 14, according to which the Israelites had to suffer forty years in the desert because of their murmuring during the forty days of the spying out of the land of Canaan. Nm 14:34 sums it up: "According to the number of the days in which you spied out the land, *forty days, for every day a year,* you shall bear your iniquity, *forty years,* and you shall know my displeasure." So it is quite natural to consider the forty days' presence of Jesus in the desert a reference to the forty years' stay of Israel in the desert.

Authors usually emphasize the relationship between Jesus and Moses fasting forty days and forty nights on Mount Sinai (Ex 34:28; Dt 9:9,18). Why does Moses not "eat bread or drink water"? Was it in preparation for the theophany? Was it because in the presence of Yahweh one need not eat normal food? In Ex 34:28 and Dt 9:9 no reason is given; in Dt 9:18 it is a vicarious penance so that Yahweh will not destroy Israel for its sins (vv. 13ff, esp. 18f): "Then I lay prostrate before the Lord as before, I neither ate bread nor drank water, because of all the sin which you had committed in doing what was evil in the sight of the Lord, to provoke him to anger. (19) For I was afraid of the anger and hot displeasure which the Lord bore against you, so that he was ready to destroy you." This last text has the best chance of being related to Mt 4:1–4/Lk 4:1–4, for the situation of Moses in Dt 9:18 is a vicarious one; he represents the people, he fasts "because of *all* the sins which you had committed." Some rabbis interpreted that to mean all the sins which the Israelites had committed during their forty-year wandering in the desert, since Dt 9 is a summary of that. This would imply that Moses fasted forty days in vicarious reparation for the forty years of Israel's sinfulness, making the comparison with Jesus even closer. One should not forget the Old Testament concept of corporate personality, whereby it is quite common for the leader, the prophet or king, to personify his people. Thus even if there is a Jesus-Moses relationship in the forty-day fast, it is not so much with Moses as distinct from Israel, but rather as representing it vicariously before Yahweh, and so the primary relationship would still be between Jesus and the Israelites in the desert.

5. Fasting and Hunger in the Desert

Both Mt and Lk use the word *epeinasen,* "he was hungry," after fasting forty days, something that was not said of Moses after his fast, nor of Elijah in 1 Kgs 19:8. In fact the rabbis, commenting on Ex 34:28, on how it was possible for a man to live without food or drink for forty days, applied the principle, "When you come into a city, act according to their customs," which meant that Moses went up "on high" where the inhabitants, the angels, do not eat, and so he did not need to eat; the angels, when they come down to earth, follow the customs of men, and eat and drink, as in Gen 18:8. Not so Jesus; he was hungry. This brings us once again to the people Israel, which also was hungry in the desert. Perhaps here, better than anywhere else, can we understand not only the existence of the Jesus-Israelites relationship, but also its significance, and with it the fundamental meaning of the first temptation of Jesus.

The people in the desert were hungry and so "tested" God, because they did not trust that he would take care of them, and because they wanted the food they craved. This is expressed clearly in Ps 78(77):17f:

17 Yet they sinned still more against him,
   rebelling against the Most High in the desert.

> 18 They tested God in their heart
>   by demanding the food they craved.

Their sin is stated again in vv.21b–22:

> 21 ... his anger mounted against Israel
> 22 because they had no faith in God,
>   and did not trust his saving power.

Then God sent them manna, v.25, but also "flesh," winged birds, v.27, so that

> 29 they ate and were filled,
>   for he gave them what they craved,

but to their destruction!
We have in these verses two reasons why the Israelites sinned against Yahweh in the desert by "testing" him: their craving and their lack of trust. Other texts also unite these ideas, e.g. Ps 106(105):13f:

> 13 But they soon forgot his works;
>   they did not wait for his counsel.
> 14 But they had a wanton craving in the wilderness
>   and put God to the test in the desert.

Craving made them forget God's works and test him by their lack of faith. Nm 11:4–6 sees strong craving as the cause of their thinking about the delicious food of Egypt and complaining about the manna; 11:34 even names the place where that happened, and where many died from eating the quails, *Qibrôt-hattaᵃwāh,* "Graves of Craving."

The relationship to the temptation of Jesus in the desert should be clear. He was hungry and the devil tempted him to satisfy that hunger in his own way, or at least to try to do so, without waiting for the Lord God to satisfy it for him. The Israelites were hungry too; they had "not eaten bread" (Dt 29:5), for the Lord had humbled them and let them hunger (Dt 8:3), to discipline them "as a man disciplines his son" (8:5), so that they would "keep the commandments of the Lord" by "walking in his ways and by fearing him" (8:6), knowing that "man does not live by bread alone, but by everything that proceeds out of the mouth of the Lord" (8:3). The Israelites failed the test. Many of them let their hunger turn into craving for the good food of Egypt and ate the quails which brought about their death at the "Graves of Craving" (Nm 11:34).

6. Stones into Bread

The suggestion of the devil that Jesus turn the stones into bread is sometimes interpreted as a request to repeat the miracle of the manna, which is on occasion called "bread" (Ex 16:12,15,22,29,32), though it is more often specified as being "bread from heaven" (Ex 16:4; Neh 9:15; Ps 105:40), or the "bread of angels" (Ps 78:25). Others rightly reject this opinion, at least at the level of Q. The parallel is not between Jesus and Moses but rather between Jesus and Israel. The manna was not converted from stones, it came from heaven, and though it nourished the Israelites sufficiently, they were not satisfied with it; they craved meat and good food from Egypt (Nm 11:6,19f; 21:5; Ps 78:18). They did not want to believe or trust in Yahweh (Ps 78:22) and committed the sin of testing him by forgetting his mighty works (Nm 14:22; Ps 78:41f; 106:13f).

The central place which Israel's sin of testing Yahweh in the desert had in later tradition underscores the principle that was being violated, namely that God, as the Creator of all things, would also care for his creatures, especially his chosen ones. He "gives food (*lehem*) to all flesh" (Ps 136:25), even to the animals (Ps 104:14), "bread to strengthen man's heart" (Ps 104:15), "food to the hungry" (Ps 146:7), to the poor (Ps 132:15), to the stranger (Dt 10:18), and especially to those who are faithful to his covenant, the upright of heart (Ex 23:25; Is 33:16; Ps 37:25).

By refusing the counsel of the devil, Jesus manifests his unshaken conviction that the Lord God would take care of him. That same trust in God's care is expressed by the comparison with a human father, who would not give his child a stone if asked for bread (Mt 7:9, possibly Q), and underlies the petition of the Lord's Prayer, "Give us this day our daily bread . . . and lead us not into temptation" (Mt 6:11–13/Lk 11:3f = Q). God is all-powerful, and can even raise "from these stones children to Abraham" (Mt 3:9/Lk 3:8 = Q).

7. Not by Bread Alone

The answer of Jesus to the devil is taken from Dt 8:3. Although Q probably only had the words of Lk 4:4, "Man shall not live by bread alone," we can assume that, as in the Talmud, the whole text was meant to be read. Mt added the rest, always following the LXX, leaving out only the last three words, "shall man live," as an unimportant repetition of the beginning. The full text belongs therefore to our discussion: "Man shall not live by bread alone, but by every word that proceeds from the mouth of God."

That which proceeds from the mouth of God, his word, is a creative vital force, absolutely firm, trustworthy, unalterable; it gives the fullness of life. The Greek *'rēma,* "word," used to translate the Hebrew expression *môṣā' pî,* "that which comes out of the mouth," in Dt 8:3, shares in the Hebrew concept of the dynamic power of God's word. Jos 21:43–45 notes that God gave Israel the land "which he swore to give to their fathers" and peace from all their enemies, and concludes, "Not one of all the good promises which the Lord had made to the house of Israel had failed; all came to pass." God's word as promise is a certainty; it never fails. Dt 8:3 stated that it would give life. Other texts echo that same assurance, e.g. Wis 16:26: ". . . that thy sons, whom thou didst love, O Lord, might learn that it is not the production of crops that feeds man, but that thy word preserves those who trust in thee"; Is 55:10f shows how that divine word is always fruitful, like a life-giving rain that makes the earth sprout, "giving seed to the sower and bread to the eater." Cf. also Prov 9:1–5; Sir 24:19–22. The author of Ps 119(118) is insistent on the need to depend on the word of God in order to live: "Thy promise gives me life" (v.50; cf. vv.107,116,154). Trust is essential, and above all, obedience. This is the meaning of the famous choice in Dt 30:19f: ". . . choose life, that you and your descendants may live, loving the Lord your God, obeying his voice."

The Israelites in the desert had been asked to entrust themselves completely to the efficacy of the divine word. They refused; Jesus accepted.

CONCLUSIONS ABOUT FASTING IN Q'S TEMPTATION NARRATIVE

According to Q, Jesus was led by the Spirit in/into the desert, did not eat for forty days, was hungry, and was then tempted by the devil to work a miracle in order to feed himself. He answered, "Man shall not live by bread alone (but by every word that proceeds from the mouth of God)."

The author of this passage in Q was intent on contrasting the attitude to God of Israel in the desert with that of Jesus. Israel was in a position of dependence and need, of hunger, even of craving; she was being tested by God to see if she would trust him and let him resolve her problem in his own way. Israel failed that test, accused God of leading her into the desert to kill her, wondered if indeed he was with her (Ex 17:7), and whether he was even able (Ps 78:20!) to give her bread. When God provided the miraculous manna for her she complained, craved the delicious food of Egypt (Nm 11:4–6) and took the first opportunity of satisfying her unruly desire for food by eating the quails, only to be punished for it at the Graves of Craving (Nm 11:34).

Jesus too was hungry. He was in a desert place, had been without food for forty days, and was tempted to turn the stone(s) into bread. But he had been led there by the Spirit. God, his Father, had put him into this situation, and would in his own time indicate what he wanted next from Jesus. No amount of hunger would make him act independently of that divine will. Jesus would find life in loving trust and obedience to God's word, knowing that concern for food was only a minor aspect of his existence, and would be taken care of by his heavenly Father.

The experience and attitude of Jesus are presented in part to explain why he did not work the kind of miracles expected of the Messiah, and bring to mind the cruel taunt hurled at him on Calvary, "If you are the Son of God, come down from the cross" (Mt 27:40), but they also have a paradigmatic significance for us. We cannot turn stones into bread, as has often been pointed out, but we could adopt the response of Israel in the desert, and from this we are warned.

In fasting we become hungry, and from that it is but a small step toward the temptation of craving and doubt. Anyone who fasts will have to come to terms with the inner motivation of the action. It is at this point that the model of Jesus inserts itself. To those tempted to consider their life primarily from the worldly vantage of eating and physical well-being, Jesus presents the way of a higher existence, of a life in which the central factor is not food but rather the word of God, accepted with faith and trust in our own divine filiation, and in his paternal care. Jesus does not teach us how long to fast—the period of forty days is not part of the paradigm, for it serves to link Jesus with ancient Israel—but he does teach us how to fast, with what inner feeling and conviction. It is our means of being still before the divine presence, led by the Spirit into the desert, and when the pangs of hunger and temptation come, we do not react to their suggestions as did Israel of old, but humbly wait in filial obedience for God's sign as to what we are to do next. He will take care of our needs in his own good time, but for the moment there is something more important for us to do, a battle to wage with the forces of selfishness and pride, of Satan, and we must become spiritually strong, overcoming those temptations that would drive a wedge between us and our heavenly Father. In fasting we come to grips with our spiritual nature; the truth that "man shall not live by bread alone" comes home to us with special force, and we are freed from the smallness of vision that is worried only about things of this world. No, true life consists for us in hearing and understanding every word that proceeds from the mouth of God, that is, considering ourselves to be addressed by the divine will, with a divine vocation to which we give ourselves in humility and trust. What that is in the concrete differs from person to person, but the fundamental attitude of listening to God and of resisting the suggestion of Satan to worry only about our own needs is a lesson that we learn from the beautiful example of Jesus, hungry and tempted in the desert.

REDACTION OF MATTHEW AND LUKE

Reconstruction of the essential features of the traditional text of Q underlying Mt 4:1-4/Lk 4:1–4 is accomplished by considering as derived from the same source (Q) whatever is in common between Mt and Lk, indicated earlier in this chapter. A redactional study of the same material picks out the differences and attempts to understand their significance in terms of the special interests manifested by the final redactor of each Gospel.[8]

Matthew

Mt 4:2 states that Jesus "fasted" whereas Lk 4:2 notes that he "ate nothing." At first glance both versions seem redactional, for the technical word *nēsteuein* in Mt betrays a special interest in fasting, while Luke's expression "ate nothing" reminds us of his style as seen by the change of Mk 2:18 "your disciples do not fast" to "yours *eat and drink*" in Lk 5:33 (and by the difference between Lk 10:7f and Mt 10:10–13). It is difficult to come to a conclusion, but if we remember that the OT background of Q is not only Dt 8:2–5 but also Ex 34:28, Dt 9:9,18, which state that Moses "*neither ate* bread nor drank water" for forty days and nights, then we can more easily accept Luke's version, "he ate nothing," as representing the original Q, and Matthew's "he fasted" as redactional. Thus Matthew deliberately changed the traditional text in order to present Jesus as "fasting" in the desert, with all the overtones of that technical word. This accords well with the other sign of a special interest in fasting on the part of the Matthean community, Mt 6:16–18, which has no parallel in Mk or Lk.

In describing the amount of time Jesus spent in the desert, Matthew says "forty days and forty nights," while Luke simply has "forty days." Matthew's expression is exactly what we find predicated of Moses on Mount Sinai, Ex 34:28; Dt 9:9, or in the desert, Dt 9:18, with the result that the redactional effect of this passage emphasizes

---

8. Cf. J. Dupont, *Les tentations de Jésus au désert* (Desclée de Brouwer, 1968) 48–53; S. Schulz, *Q. Die Spruchquelle,* 177–190.

the link between Jesus and Moses. That same allusion appears in Mt 4:8, the temptation of Jesus on "a very high mountain," and 5:1, the setting of the Sermon on the Mount. In contrast, Luke de-emphasizes the Moses motif by eliminating the mountain in the temptation scenes completely, substituting for it a "moment of time" (Lk 4:5), and by staging his version of Mt 5:1ff in the plain (Lk 6:17).

Another redactional element in Matthew is the designation of the devil as "the tempter" (4:3), 'o peirazōn, a present participle of the verb *peirazein,* which links our passage with Mt 16:1; 19:3; 22:18; 22:35, where the same verb is used of the opponents of Jesus, thereby associating temptation by the devil with that of the Sadducees and Pharisees, especially the latter.

In quoting the answer of Jesus to the devil, Luke merely gives the first part of Dt 8:3 LXX, "Man shall not live by bread alone," while Matthew completes the citation, "but by every word that proceeds from the mouth of God." Matthew emphasizes a little more the importance of the word of God as a source of life.

Of significance too are the words with which Jesus dismisses the devil in Mt 4:10, "Begone, Satan," 'upage satana, the very words of Jesus to Peter in 16:23 (though there Jesus adds "behind me," to soften the tone). This may well be an intensification of Q's reflection on the nature of Jesus' messianic mission, which includes suffering and death instead of the establishment of a political kingdom (see our remarks on the *Sitz im Leben* of the whole passage).

Finally, Matthew takes over from Mk 1:13 the service of the angels at the end of the temptations, 4:11, "and angels . . . ministered to him": the angels fed Jesus after his fast.

As regards fasting, we conclude that Matthew wanted to emphasize the importance of fasting by clearly portraying the forty-day stay of Jesus in the desert as a fast. Q had already presented Jesus as a contrast to the Israelites in the desert; Matthew slightly expanded that picture by making the reference to Moses more explicit. The introduction of the angels in Mt 4:11 showed the divine approbation of Jesus' fast; as a reward, he is fed by angels.

Luke

An especially significant redactional element in Lk 4:1–4 is the phrase "full of the Holy Spirit" (4:1). In the whole New Testament this expression appears only here and three times in Acts (6:5; 7:55; 11:24). It refers back to the baptism of Jesus at which, according to Lk 3:23 (diff. Mt 3:16 and Mk 1:10) the "Holy Spirit" descended upon him. That same intention explains the reference to the Jordan in Lk 4:1. The Christians too were baptized by the Holy Spirit (Lk 3:16), so Luke seems to hint that just as Jesus was baptized, full of the Holy Spirit, and yet tempted, the Christians too must face temptation. Other redactional elements confirm this. In 4:13 Luke notes that the devil departed from Jesus "until an opportune time," preparing the way for his return, as he does in 22:3,53. Indeed, according to Luke, the temptation of Jesus will continue in his disciples: Lk 22:28,31,40,46; Acts 5:3; 13:10.

Contrary to Mt and Mk, Luke inserts the genealogy of Jesus (Lk 3:23–38) between the baptism and temptation scenes. The genealogy itself presents Jesus as the son of Adam (diff. Mt 1:1ff), the classical example of one who was tempted. Adam fell; Jesus did not.

In Lk too the first temptation is rooted in the fact of Jesus' hunger, and the suggestion of the devil is aimed at having Jesus satisfy his own hunger by working a miracle. Luke even corrects the plural "stones" to the singular in order to make the scene more realistic, for Jesus would need only one loaf of bread to satisfy his hunger. Luke remains faithful to the fundamental insights of Q, and Jesus is presented also in Lk as a counter-figure to the Israel of Dt 8:2–5.

Yet where Mt has added touches to enhance the importance of fasting, and of the figure of Moses, Luke has chosen to emphasize the identification of Jesus with the newly baptized Christians, led by the Spirit, but subject to temptation, as Adam was.

HISTORICITY IN THE LIFE OF JESUS

The question of the historical reality of the temptations of Jesus as portrayed in Mt 4:1–11/Lk 4:1–13 is dependent upon an accurate appraisal of the *Sitz im Leben* of the text of Q, and of its relationship to other texts that speak of the temptations of Jesus, especially Mk 1:12f.

We have already characterized the literary genre of Q's temptation narrative as a "scribal haggada," for the reasons given above, and have therefore denied the historicity of the narrative as such. Yet there still remains the problem of origin. What social and theological situation best explains how the story came to be formed? Was it a spiritual experience of Jesus that he later told the disciples? Was it made up to show why Jesus did not perform magic-like miracles? Or was it not rather an account formed by someone in the early Christian community to explain why Jesus did not conform to the popular image of a Messiah who would set up his kingdom and free Israel from foreign domination?

We have seen that the account presents Jesus in contrast to ancient Israel; where Israel failed through disobedience and lack of trust, Jesus succeeded. Jesus is the new Israel, Son of God, and manifests his sonship through unswerving obedience to the will of his Father. He is thus an example for the Christians, although certain presuppositions, such as his ability to turn stones into bread or offer to receive dominion over the whole world, show that more was involved. This other aspect centers on the nature of his messianic calling. It amounted to no less than a rejection of the political conception of the Messiah! Schlatter pointed out that though the narrative was not directly concerned with messianic considerations, it nevertheless put aside "popular ideas about the Messiah."[9] I believe that is correct.

Bultmann's opinion that the account was directed against a magical misuse of Jesus' power to work miracles, with its underlying acceptance of the Hellenistic concept of Jesus as a miracle-working *theios anēr,* is too shortsighted. The actions demanded of Jesus by the devil do not fall completely under the heading of typically Hellenistic wonders. It may perhaps be true of the request to turn stones into bread, but it does not explain worship of the devil in order to rule over all the kingdoms of the world, nor even the suggestion to hurl himself from the pinnacle, for Jesus was not asked to work a miracle;

9. A. Schlatter, *Der Evangelist Matthäus* (Stuttgart: Calwer, 1929) 111.

the presumption was that, according to Ps 91, the angels would come and carry him in their arms.

The background is a Jewish one, and deals with the problem of messianic expectations. Some authors, notably J. Jeremias and J. Dupont, insist that this was an issue only in the life of Jesus, which was resolved for the Christians by his death and resurrection. Therefore the temptation narrative has its natural explanation only in the situation of Jesus, and goes back to him.[10] Others[11] admit that it certainly was a concern during the life of Jesus, as recent studies on the Zealot movement have emphasized, but the same situation obtained also after the resurrection. The primitive Palestinian community did not simply lead an internal life such as described in Acts 2:42–47, waiting for Jesus' return (1 Thess 1:10); they also had to take a stance toward the religious and political movements for independence from Rome which led to the siege and destruction of Jerusalem in 70 A.D. The ideology of the Zealots had heavy religious, especially apocalyptic overtones; the same was true of Qumran. Why then did the Christians not join these anti-Roman independence forces if they recognized Jesus as the Messiah who was to come? The temptation narrative supplies the answer. It was not the will of God, but rather a satanic temptation. Just as Jesus served God alone, waiting in trust for him to supply his needs, so the Christian community would do the same.

It would then be simplest to suppose that a learned scribe in the Christian community, meditating on the parallels between Jesus and ancient Israel in the light of Dt 6—8 and of the messianic expectations that were centered to a large extent in the desert, the Temple, and world domination, constructed the haggada of the temptation narrative.

A similar non-historical origin must be posited also for Mk 1:12f. Dupont lists seven different opinions as to the relationship between Mt 4:1–11/Lk 4:1–13 and Mk 1:12f, and concludes that the texts represent two parallel traditions, two different versions which treat of the temptation of Jesus in the desert from at least partially

---

10. Dupont, *Les tentations,* 127–129; J. Jeremias, *TDNT* IV, 868, note 224.
11. Gerhardsson, *The Testing of God's Son,* 11–13; P. Hoffmann, "Die Versuchungsgeschichte in der Logienquelle," *BZ* 13 (1969) 207–223, esp.213f.

divergent points of view.[12] Mk 1:12f does not intend to relate a bio-graphical fact in the life of Jesus, but rather a theological truth about his status as a new Adam.

Other texts, however, such as Mk 3:22–27 par, Mk 8:33 par, Mt 13:24–30, Lk 22:31, and the various accounts of exorcisms reflect much more accurately the historical situation of Jesus' battle with the devil and serve as a solid substratum for the accounts of Mk 1:12 and Mt 4:1–11/Lk 4:1–13.

CONCLUSION

As we try to ascertain the contribution of this account toward a biblical theology of fasting, we must note carefully what it intends to say, aware of the danger of falsifying the text by asking questions of it which it was not designed to answer.

In both Mt and Lk the temptation comes immediately after the baptism of Jesus. The Spirit descends upon him, and he is declared the beloved Son in whom the Father is well pleased. Since it is the Spirit which leads him into the desert, it is an action willed by God. It precedes his public ministry, and functions as an immediate intro-duction to it. According to Mt, Jesus fasts for forty days and nights. This should not be taken as a preparation for divine revelation, for none follows. No reason is given for the fast, except perhaps the *peir-asthēnai* of v.1, "in order to be tempted." That, however, and the general context, as we have seen above, points to the correlation be-tween the action of Jesus and that of the Israelites in the desert, ac-cording to Dt 8:2–5. Jesus is one with the Israelites, through his fasting in the desert, which then gave rise to his hunger, and the temptation. Jesus overcame that temptation by noting that man does not live by bread alone.

I think the value of this passage for a proper understanding of Christian fasting lies precisely here. Fasting is presented as a means of solidarity with the hungry and the tempted, and as a lesson that a person does not live by bread alone. It puts one into temptation of craving, but places him/her also into the presence of God, and al-lows him/her to become aware of the overriding importance of every

12. Dupont, 85–93.

word that proceeds from God's mouth, namely, of the divine will. It is a terrifying but awesome action in which one confronts personal weakness and divine presence at the same time. The example of Jesus teaches the proper reaction: trust and obedience. God is the Lord of history, and in his own way will care for his beloved children, his chosen ones.

The account in Luke does not differ radically from that of Matthew. Here too Jesus did not eat anything "in those (forty) days," was hungry, tempted, and overcame the temptation by reflecting that man does not live by bread alone. Human weakness gave way to fidelity.

CHAPTER FIVE

Almsgiving, Prayer, and Fasting (Mt 6:1–18)

If we look for a common unifying "golden thread" in the writings of the Church Fathers about fasting we would find it in their unanimous encouragement of the practice, but in conjunction with the twin virtues of prayer and almsgiving.[1] The author of the *Shepherd of Hermas* (III,7) recommended giving to a widow or orphan the amount of money saved by fasting.[2] Origen, in his *Homilies on Leviticus* (10,2) blessed those who would fast "in order to nourish the poor."[3] St. Augustine, who wrote a whole book on fasting, felt that to fast without giving away what one would otherwise have eaten was an expression of avarice, for in effect one was simply saving it for the following day.[4] St. Leo the Great, justly famous for his many sermons on fasting, declared: "There are three things which most belong to religious actions, namely prayer, fasting, and almsgiving,"[5] and St. Peter Chrysologus said: "Prayer, helping the needy, fasting—these three things are really one; fasting is the soul of prayer, and helping the needy is the life-blood of fasting."[6]

---

1. A. Guillaume, *Jeûne et charité dans l'Eglise latine, des origines au XIIe siècle, en particulier chez saint Léon le Grand* (Paris: Laboureur et Companie, 1954).

2. Quoted in "Jeûne, Appendice: Dossier patristique sur le jeûne," *Dictionnaire de Spiritualité* VIII, 1177.

3. Cited in Paul VI's Apostolic Constitution *Poenitemini, AAS* 58,3 (Feb. 1966) 192, n. 53.

4. Sermon 208, *Fathers of the Church* 38 (New York: Fathers of the Church, Inc., 1959) 92–93.

5. Sermon 12,4; *ML* 54,171, cited in *Poenitemini,* 194.

6. Sermon 43; *Dictionnaire de Spiritualité,* VIII,1177.

The relationship between almsgiving, prayer, and fasting has been a fruitful one throughout the ages. Its roots go back to the Old Testament, but its most precise formulation is first found in Mt 6:2–6, 16–18.

This passage has no parallels in Mark or Luke. One might suspect that it was composed by the final redactor of Mt, but there are indications that it was formed previously. Mt 6:2–4,5f,16–18 is a perfectly symmetrical triptych on almsgiving, prayer, and fasting which was later interrupted by the insertion of vv 7–15 on the Our Father.[7]

The final redactor of Mt did not compose vv 2–6,16–18, for it is hardly probable that he would have formed such a fine parallel between the sections on almsgiving, prayer, and fasting only in order to destroy it by inserting, with introduction and parenetic conclusion, the liturgical prayer of his community, the Our Father. We do not know whether he was the one who introduced the Our Father into the pre-existent unit 6:2–4,5f,16–18 or whether the two passages were already joined together in his sources.

In order to understand the meaning of fasting in Mt 6:16–18 at the three levels of redaction, previous tradition, and historicity in the life of Jesus, we will have to consider the pericope from a threefold point of view:

(a) *level of redaction:* we must study especially 6:1, written most probably by the final editor, and also the place of 6:2–18 in the structure of the Sermon on the Mount;

(b) *level of previous tradition:* we must consider Mt 6:2–4,5f,16–18 as a unit;

(c) *level of the historical Jesus:* using the various criteria of ascertaining the historicity of the words of Jesus, we shall arrive at a probable conclusion.

TRADITION

I will treat the various levels of composition by beginning with the middle one, that of the formation of Mt 6:2–4,5f,16–18 as a unit

---

7. J. O'Hara, "Christian Fasting (Mt 6:16–18)," *Scripture* 19 (1967) 3–18; A. George, "La justice à faire dans le secret (Matthieu 6,1–6 et 16–18)," *Bib* 40 (1959) 590–598. Authors agree almost unanimously that vv 1–6,16–18 once formed a unit.

before its introduction into the Gospel of Matthew. We have already seen that it was formed prior to its inclusion in the Gospel.

Why is there a three-part unity on almsgiving, prayer, and fasting? It is generally pointed out that these activities summarize the Jewish ideals of piety as expressed in some of the later books of the Old Testament as well as in the Talmud. Bousset-Gressmann called them the "fundamental pillars of the Jewish religion,"[8] Bonnard speaks of the "three fundamental Jewish practices,"[9] and Schweizer calls them "the three most important demonstrations of religious devotion in Judaism."[10] Yet when they look for citations that group almsgiving, prayer, and fasting as a unity, authors have more difficulty than they would like to admit. W.D. Davies states that "this collocation, though not completely and not exactly in this order, is a common one in Judaism," but none of the examples that he gives is convincing.[11] Sir 7:8–10 has no mention of fasting, nor does Tobit 12:7–9, which he reads as "better is prayer with truth and alms with righteousness . . . ," nor is it immediately clear that of the triad in T.J. Ta'anit ii.1 the last word, *šwbh*, literally "repentance," means fasting. B. Gerhardsson sees the triad in the *šᵉma'* of Dt 6:4f, which commands love of God with one's whole heart, soul, and strength (Mammon = possessions), but that does not convince either.[12]

Authors often cite Tob 12:8 as containing a reference to the triad "almsgiving, prayer, and fasting," and in fact the shorter LXX codices A and B do read: "Prayer is better when accompanied by fasting, almsgiving, and justice." But scholars are now more inclined to accept the reading of the longer LXX manuscript S which does not mention fasting: "Prayer is good when accompanied by truth,

8. W. Bousset and H. Gressmann, *Die Religion des Judentums im späthellenistischen Zeitalter*⁴ (Tübingen: Mohr, 1966) 181.

9. P. Bonnard, *L'Evangile selon saint Matthieu*² (Neuchatel: Delachaux & Niestlé, 1970) 77.

10. E. Schweizer, *The Good News According to Matthew* (Atlanta: John Knox Press, 1975) 139.

11. W.D. Davies, *The Setting of the Sermon on the Mount* (Cambridge: University Press, 1966) 308.

12. B. Gerhardsson, "Geistiger Opferdienst nach Matth 6,1–6,16–21," *Neues Testament und Geschichte*. Festschr. für O. Cullmann, ed. by H. Baltensweiler *et al.* (Zürich/Tübingen: Theologischer Verlag/Mohr, 1972) 73f.

and almsgiving with righteousness is better than wealth with unrighteousness." Aramaic and Hebrew fragments of the Book of Tobit were found in cave four of Qumran, and they helped confirm the opinion that the longer manuscript S gives the original semitic (Aramaic?) rendering better than the shorter MSS A and B, which seem to reflect an abridgement by a Hellenistic redactor.[13] So at the very least, the original mention of fasting in Tob 12:8 is highly doubtful, and we cannot find here a neat expression of the triad in Mt 6:2–4,5f,16–18.

The Book of Tobit, written about 200 B.C., is nevertheless important as a general background to Mt 6. The practice of prayer and almsgiving is mentioned as a unit in 12:8, and these virtues are also emphasized elsewhere: the example of prayer is given in 3:1–6,11–15; 8:4–8, and is recommended in 4:19; almsgiving is enjoined in 4:7–11,16; 14:11, and in 14:2 it is pointed out that Tobit "gave alms, and continued to fear the Lord and to praise him." Tob 2:4 and 12:13 might also serve as examples of fasting.

Similar concern about almsgiving, prayer, and fasting is found also in the Book of Sirach, written in Hebrew about 180 B.C. Some fragments of the Hebrew text were found at Qumran, although the bulk of the Hebrew text we have today comes from the Cairo Geniza, found between 1896 and 1900. It was translated into Greek by Jesus ben-Sirach's grandson. Almsgiving is recommended in 3:29—4:10; 7:32–36; 29:8–13, and in 7:10 it is mentioned along with prayer: "Do not be fainthearted in your prayer nor neglect to give alms"; the example of prayer is given in 50:22–24, and is recommended also in 39:15. Sir 34:26 mentions fasting together with prayer, and emphasizes the need for interior conversion and firm purpose of amendment: "So if a man fasts for his sins, and goes again and does the same things, who will listen to his prayer? And what has he gained by humbling himself?"

Almsgiving, prayer, and fasting, as concepts, appear in Is 58:4–10. The text concerns true fasting and mentions almsgiving as the need to "share your bread with the hungry and bring the homeless

---

13. P.W. Skehan, "The Scrolls and the OT Text," *New Directions in Biblical Archaeology,* ed. by D.N. Freedman and J.C. Greenfield (New York: 1971) 111; the *vetus latina* reading of Tob 12:8 does not include fasting either.

into your house, and when you see the naked to cover him" (v.7); this will then make your prayer effective: "Then you shall call, and the Lord will answer . . ." (v.9). These three concepts can be found as well in the Testament of Joseph 3,1–6, which reads in part: ". . . going into my chamber, I wept and prayed unto the Lord. And I fasted in those seven years . . . and for three days I did not take my food, but I gave it to the poor and sick."[14]

Actually, in spite of the lack of a single text which simply lists all three practices, almsgiving, prayer, and fasting have a long history in Israel, as is seen by references in many parts of the Old Testament. *Alsmgiving,* caring for the poor and giving them gratuitously what they need, is a fundamental tenet of the Torah. The sabbatical year of Ex 23:10f meant keeping the fields fallow "so that the poor of your people may eat; and what they leave, the wild beasts may eat"; Lev 23:22 decreed that one must not reap the harvest to the very border of the fields, nor gather the gleanings, but rather to "leave them for the poor and for the stranger"; the same thought is expressed in Dt 24:19–22, and a general exhortation to lend freely, even as the sabbatical year, the "year of release," is approaching, is expressed in Dt 15:7–11. *Prayer* is the soul of the Old Testament, and its most important aspect, worship, is expressed in the very first commandment, "You shall have no other gods before me" (Ex 20:3). The Book of Psalms illustrates quite clearly how well it was carried out, not only publicly, but also privately in one's room: "My mouth praises thee with joyful lips, when I think of thee upon my bed, and meditate on thee in the watches of the night . . ." (Ps 63:6f). *Fasting* too goes back to the early days of Israel's history, the period of the Judges and Kings (Jgs 20:26; 1 Sam 7:6; 14:24–29; 28:20–23; 31:13). It is an essential ingredient of the Day of Atonement (Lev 16; 23:26–32), and increased in intensity after the Exile, becoming especially common in late Judaism.

We have been referring to almsgiving, prayer, and fasting as practices of "piety," while yet insisting that they stem from fidelity to the Law, which is summed up in the word "justice," and in fact Mt 6:1 considers these practices as examples of *dikaiosunē.* Is there a distinction between piety and justice, or are they two expressions for

14. R.H. Charles, ed., *Pseudepigrapha* (Oxford: Clarendon Press, 1913) 347.

the same reality? Later Rabbinic Judaism made a distinction between the *ṣaddiq,* "just," and the *ḥâsid,* "pious"; the first observed the Law; the second applied himself to good works over and above the Law, as portrayed especially in the Book of Tobit.

This distinction helps to explain the whole difference of mentality between the Pharisees and the Sadducees; the Pharisees (whose origins are tied up with those of the *Ḥasidim*) tended to extend the application of the Law even to cases not specifically prescribed, and then added other customs to safeguard the Law, while the Sadducees (whose very name is connected, according to some commentators, with the word *ṣaddiq*) tended to interpret the Law very strictly and to limit its application as much as possible. As regards almsgiving, prayer, and fasting, both groups would have had to practice them, but to a different extent. The distinction is more one of degree than one of kind.

In conclusion, we have seen that although the practices of almsgiving, prayer, and fasting are ancient and pertain to the Law as well as to expressions of piety, the threefold grouping of these acts was not frequent in the Old Testament, and there is no text which clearly influenced the triadic composition of Mt 6:2–4,5f,16–18. This points to the originality of the author.

LITERARY GENRE OF MT 6:2–4,5f,16–18

The literary genre employed in this passage is a catechesis, simple, easy to learn by heart. Bultmann classified it under the heading "Legal Sayings and Church Rules" and referred to its character of a "Church catechism."[15] He termed Mt 6:2–6,16–18 "Rules of Piety" (along with Mt 5:23f; 23:16–22; Mk 11:25; Lk 17:3f) which express the piety characteristic of the community as distinct from Judaism. He added that this was true even if these rules have their Jewish parallels. In tracing the general history of this material, Bultmann pointed out that the sayings of Jesus which are formulated in a legal style tend to be older, and although their form comes essentially from the

---

15. R. Bultmann, *The History of the Synoptic Tradition*[2] (Oxford: Blackwell, 1972) 133, n.l.

community, their content does not.[16] M. Albertz called these verses a didactic poem;[17] H. Betz refers to them as a "cult didache,"[18] and van Tilborg defines them as a "Christian halacha" influenced by the genre of wisdom literature.[19] All of these titles emphasize the religiously didactic nature of the text.

What is the immediate background against which Mt 6:2-4, 5f,16-18 was formed? What social situation does it most accurately reflect? In order to answer these questions we will have to make an analysis of the passage as a whole, of its structure, and then of its salient parts. In view of our special interest in fasting, there will be a closer examination of vv 16-18.

There is an astonishingly identical pattern to each of the paragraphs on almsgiving (vv 2-4), prayer (vv 5f), and fasting (vv 16-18). All are divided into two parts, the first (A), negative, not to be like the "hypocrites," and the second (B), positive, what to do instead. Each of these sections, A and B, is then subdivided into four units:

1. indication of the act of piety;
2. description of how it should (or should not) be performed;
3. explicit mention of motive;
4. statement about a reward.

Let us now examine the individual parts of the structure.

1. Indication of the Act of Piety (negative, 6:2a,5a,16a; positive, 6:3a,6a,17a).

The first thing to notice is that fasting is on exactly the same footing as almsgiving and prayer; all three are recommended. What is condemned is a certain manner of carrying them out.

---

16. *Ibid.,* 146f.
17. Cited by Bultmann, 133, n.l.
18. H.D. Betz, "Eine judenchristliche Kult-Didache in Matthäus 6,1–18," *Jesus Christus in Historie und Geschichte,* Festschr. for H. Conzelmann, ed. by G. Strecker (Tübingen: Mohr, 1975) 445–457.
19. S. van Tilborg, *The Jewish Leaders in Matthew* (Leiden: Brill, 1972) 11f.

A SCHEMATIC FORM

A. NEGATIVE DESCRIPTION

1. *Indication of the act of piety:*
   6:3a—when you (s) give alms
   6:5a—and when you (pl) pray
   6:16a—and when you (pl) fast

2. *Polemical description of the ostentatious manner of the "hypocrites":*
   6:2b—sound no trumpet before you, as the hypocrites do in the synagogues and in the streets
   6:5b—you must not be like the hypocrites; for they love to stand and pray in the synagogues and at the street corners
   6:16b—do not look dismal like the hypocrites, for they disfigure their faces

3. *Explicit mention of their worldly motive:*
   6:2c—that they may be praised by men
   6:5c—that they may be seen by men
   6:16c—that their fasting may be seen by men.

4. *Ironical statement that they have received their reward:*
   6:2d—Amen, I say to you (pl), they have received their reward
   6:5d—Amen, I say to you (pl), they have received their reward
   6:16d—Amen, I say to you (pl), they have received their reward

B. POSITIVE DESCRIPTION

1. *Indication of the act of piety:*
   6:3a—but when you (s) give alms
   6:6a—but when you (s) pray
   6:17a—but when you (s) fast

2. *Hyperbolic description of the correct manner of performing the act:*
   6:3b—do not let your left hand know what your right hand is doing
   6:6b—go into your room and shut the door
   6:17b—anoint your head and wash your face

3. *Mention of secrecy as motive for carrying it out this way:*
   6:4a—so that your alms may be in secret
   6:6b—pray to your Father who is in secret
   6:18a—so that your fasting may not be seen by men but by your Father who is in secret

4. *Promise of future reward from the Father:*
   6:4b—and your Father who sees in secret will reward you
   6:6c—and your Father who sees in secret will reward you
   6:18b—and your Father who sees in secret will reward you

Who is addressed?

The person to whom these acts of piety are recommended is "you," in the singular for almsgiving ("when *thou* givest alms"; 6:2a;3a), but in the plural for the negative sections on prayer and fasting ("and when *ye* pray," 6:5a; "and when *ye* fast," 6:16a), followed by a singular in the sections that deal with the positive commands ("but when *thou* prayest," 6:6a; "but when *thou* dost fast," 6:17a).

Extending the discussion of the change between the second person singular and plural to the whole pericope, we note the following:

The paragraph on almsgiving (6:2–4) begins with a singular ("when *thou* givest alms") and continues in the singular ("sound no trumpet before *thee*"), switches to the plural in the Amen-formula ("Amen, I say to *ye*"), returns to the singular in the positive part ("but when *thou* givest alms") and maintains the singular in the final reward-saying ("*thy* Father . . . will reward *thee*"). Thus all of it is addressed to a "thou" in the singular, with the exception of the Amen-formula.

The paragraph on prayer (6:5f) begins with a "you" plural ("when *ye* pray"), continues with it for the negative part ("be *ye* not like the hypocrites"), including the Amen-formula ("Amen, I say to *ye*"). Then, in the positive section, the text switches to the singular ("but when *thou* prayest, go into *thy* room . . . pray to *thy* Father") and remains in the singular throughout, including the reward-saying ("and *thy* Father . . . will reward *thee*").

The paragraph on fasting (6:16–18) begins likewise with a "you" plural ("and when *ye* fast"), continues the plural in the negative section ("do *ye* not look dismal"), including the Amen-formula ("Amen, I say to *ye*"). The positive section is then in the singular ("but when *thou* fastest, anoint *thy* head and wash *thy* face, so that *thy* fasting may not be seen by men"), and concludes in the singular with the final reward-saying ("and *thy* Father who sees in secret will reward *thee*").

The switch from the second person singular to plural in this passage has been well explained by Gerhardsson,[20] who sees it as a sign

20. Gerhardsson, "Geistiger Opferdienst," 71.

that the text was addressed to a group, not as a whole, but rather as to individuals within that group. Each member of the assembly was addressed singly, in a personal way, while yet being a member of the group. This is especially true in the latter positive commands, which address the individual's sense of discretion.

This use of "you" is characteristic of catechetical literature, of directives given to whoever would accept them, to "students" or "disciples"; the second person singular predominates, but the plural is there with it, side by side, showing that all the members of the group are addressed, but each one individually.

2. Polemical Description of the Ostentatious Manner of the 'Hypocrites' (negative description, 6:2b,5b,16b), and Hyperbolic Description of Correct Manner in Performing the Act (positive description, 6:3b,6b,17b).

The initial verbs which begin these descriptions of the incorrect and correct manner of performing the works of piety are in the imperative mood, or in the future or subjunctive with imperative force: almsgiving: "sound no trumpet"; prayer: "be not like (the hypocrites)"; fasting: "do not look dismal"; and on the positive side, almsgiving: "let not (your left hand) know"; prayer: "go (into your room)"; fasting: "anoint (your head)." These imperatives show that we are dealing with an instruction, with advice: "don't do that, do this!" The descriptions of what is to be avoided or what is to be done are from the very beginning conditioned by these imperatives. They are not mere declarative portrayals of how certain people act. They are formed almost as caricatures, to show clearly how foolish and wrong it would be to act that way. The descriptions are exaggerated, both as to what is to be avoided and as to what is to be done.

Commentators have not found any clear example of people sounding the trumpet when they give alms. As for standing in the street corners to pray, that was common, not necessarily in order to be seen, but because there were Jewish sacrifices at certain times of the day, and the people wanted to participate in them by prayer at those times, wherever they were. Muslims today still act in a similar way. In the case of fasting, the choice of the verb *aphanizō*, "disfigure," may well have been determined not by a desire to give an accurate description of how some men fast but rather in order to form a play on words: "they disfigure (*aphanizousin*) their faces that they may appear (*phanōsin*) to men as fasting." Again, we have no record as to how one would "disfigure" his/her face in order to appear as fasting.

The same exaggeration appears in the description of the right way of doing things. It is impossible for the left hand not to know what the right is doing; it is highly unlikely that the only kind of prayer that was recommended was prayer in a closet or inner room, and it seems unreal that one should anoint his/her head while fasting, something that was forbidden on the Day of Atonement, and which would in any case attract attention. These are (merely) picturesque descriptions with a catechetical purpose. The exaggerated tone helps to bring home the real point of the lesson: don't look for human praise when you do these things; do them for God alone.

We may ask, are these only pictures, theoretical examples of universal application, or are real people, certain members of the community, described by the word "hypocrites" and by the illustrations of sounding a horn when giving alms, praying in public in order to be seen by others, and looking dismal when fasting so that others will notice the pain?

In the context of the Gospel according to Matthew, there can be little doubt that the "hypocrites" of 6:2,5,16 are the same people as the "scribes and Pharisees, hypocrites" of Mt 23:13,15,23,25,27,29, the "scribes and Pharisees" of 23:2 who do all their deeds "to be seen by men" (23:5); cf 6:1! This will be discussed when we reach the level of the Matthean redaction. But if we dissociate Mt 6:2–4,5f,16–18 from 6:1 and treat it as an independent unit of tradition, then we will have to decide on the basis of the structure of the text itself, of its literary genre, and work out its original *Sitz im Leben* as distinct from its *Sitz in der Redaktion*.

So far we have a plural audience, addressed singly, in the imperative or equivalent. The subject is basic works of piety, and the style is exhortatory. There are exaggerations in order to make a point very clear. Perhaps it is helpful at this stage to review briefly the conclusions of exegetes on the literary genre of this text. They emphasize its catechetical, that is, its instructional, character. They speak of a "community catechism" (Bultmann), a "didactic poem" (Albertz), a "cultic teaching" (Betz), a "Christian halachah" influenced by wisdom literature (van Tilborg). It would seem to be characteristic of the genre itself that the examples given be general, of universal application, theoretical and illustrative, rather than real. In other words, the description of the "hypocrites" who act in order to be praised by men, and who have therefore already received their reward, is not a character sketch of certain people in the community, such as the scribes and Pharisees, but rather a negative model, a portrayal of what one ought not to be. In fact, the word 'upokritēs receives its best definition here; what is a "hypocrite"? It is one who sounds a horn when giving alms, one who prays and fasts in such a way so as to be seen!

It seems then that the "hypocrites" of Mt 6:2–4,5f,16–18 are not specifically the scribes and Pharisees, at the level of oral tradition, but rather catechetical "straw men" who form the negative backdrop of the positive teaching on how to give alms, pray and fast.[21]

3. Explicit Mention of Motive (negative: 6:2c,5c,16c; positive: 6:4a,6b,18a).

Not only is the external manner of almsgiving, prayer, and fasting clearly contrasted between that of the "hypocrites" and "you"; the inner motive is also explicitly stated in each case: they, "in order to be praised by men" (6:2c) or "in order to be seen by men" (6:5c,16c); you, so that your acts of piety may be performed "in secret" (6:4a) or before "your Father who is in secret" (6:6b,18a). This contrast of motivation was already implicit in the description of the external actions; the fact that it is now explicitly stated means that it was most important to the author and constitutes the central affirmation of his teaching. Everything has been leading up to this, and everything else devolves from it. Even the final statement on reward, important as it is in its own right, is subordinated to the central con-

---

21. P. Minear, "False Prophecy and Hypocrisy in the Gospel of Matthew," *Neues Testament und Kirche,* Festschrift for R. Schnackenburg, ed. by J. Gnilka (Freiburg: Herder, 1974) 79, points out that Matthew wanted to encourage faithfulness on the part of the Christian leaders, and therefore presented the scribes and Pharisees as an "image of villainy" not to be imitated.

cern of teaching about purity of motive, as the repetition of the expression "in secret" (6:4b,6c,18b) shows.

Acts of piety are to be performed solely and exclusively for the Lord, or, rather, for "your Father who is in secret." No secondary glance toward one's reputation in the estimation of men is allowed. Not only is the total and unique sovereignty of the Lord emphasized—the very inner definition of the religious person is hinted at. This is brought out especially by the contrast between "in the sight of men" (6:5c,16c) and "before your Father" (6:6b,18a). In the Bible a person is authenticated by the judgment of God, by how he/she appears "before him," in the Old Testament—Gen 3:8; 4:14; 19:13; Ex 20:3; Hos 7:2; Jon 1:3—and in the New—Mt 10:32f; 25:32; 2 Cor 5:10.[22] We are here at the very heart of true religion.

The expression for God, "thy Father who is in secret," is also significant. *Patēr sou,* "thy Father," referring to God as the Father of someone other than Jesus, is found nowhere else in the New Testament, only here (Mt 6:4b,6bc,18ab).[23] In the Old Testament it is found only in Dt 32:6. It emphasizes the intimate, personal character of the relationship between God and his child, each one in a group taken singly. The closeness of the relationship is brought out already in Dt 32:6, where the primary aspect, the Father as authority who judges, also appears.

The passage in Deuteronomy points once again to the sapiential character of Mt 6:2–6,16–18, for the immediate context of Dt 32:6 is also sapiential.

Although there are interesting points of similarity, the difference between the use of the expression "thy Father" in Dt 32:6 and Mt 6:4,6,18 is illuminating. Deuteronomy reflects the Old Testament concept of God as Father of the chosen people, and the "thy" of "thy Father" in Dt 32:6 refers to the "people." In Mt 6 it is no longer the "people"; it is the disciple who looks neither to the right nor to the left while carrying out religious duties in the presence of his Father,

22. Bonnard, *Matthieu,* 78.
23. The expression "thy Father" appears also in Lk 15:27, as part of a parable, and thus only indirectly of God as Father. The parable is important for its emphasis on the closeness of God to his children, but it does not take away from the uniqueness of the expression in Mt 6. Cf. also 1 Cor 4:5 and 1 Pet 3:4.

alone. The New Testament teaching on God as Father has broken away from the group emphasis and directs its thought to the personal relationship between the individual and God in a very intimate way.[24] This is expressed most powerfully by the use of *abba,* "Daddy" (Mk 14:36; Rom 8:15), but the same familiarity is found in the expression "thy Father" of these verses which portray the personal relationship between God and his child in a context of uniqueness of motive and assurance of reward; it may even hint at the nature of the reward—closer union.

In Secret

The ancient Hebrews were aware that things done in secret were not hidden from God—Jer 23:24; 49:10; Ez 8:12; Ps 33:13–19; 139:7–17; Qo 12:14; Sir 1:30; 17:15; 23:18f; 39:19—but the emphasis was on the certain punishment of secret sins rather than on reward for hidden acts of virtue. At best one has the inclusive category that God knows everything, the good along with the bad, as in Ps 33; 139; Qo 12:14; Sir 39:19, but the idea of performing good works before his secret gaze alone is hardly alluded to in the Old Testament. Of course the prophets wanted their people to serve the Lord with pure heart—Hos 3:2; 6:3; Jer 17:9f; 31:33f; Ez 36:26f—but here too the emphasis was on the true practice of virtue, as opposed to sin, rather than on the hiddenness of the virtuous acts themselves in order to be performed for God alone.[25]

Josephus bears witness to that same Old Testament mentality. Schlatter[26] quotes several passages from his works as an illustration of Mt 6:4, "who sees in secret," namely *Ant* 6,263–265; 9:3; and *Wars* 5,413, but three of the four passages speak about crimes committed in secret, and the fourth, *Ant* 9,3, is a warning given by Josaphat to judges that they should judge justly, "for God sees every one

24. G. Bornkamm, *Jesus of Nazareth* (New York: Harper & Row, 1960) 124–129. On occasion the Old Testament used the term Father to express closeness to God, but only rarely, and then mostly in prayer of petition: Is 63:16; 64:7; Jer 3:19; 31:9; Sir 23:1; 51:10. Rabbinic literature uses it more frequently, especially in commentaries on Dt 32:6 and Is 64:7; cf. Strack-Billerbeck I, 393–396.

25. Cf. kruptō, *TDNT* III, 967–971.

26. A. Schlatter, *Der Evangelist Matthäus* (Stuttgart: Calwer, 1929) 201f.

of those works performed secretly." None of these passages treats the point at issue—that good works are to be performed not for the approval of men but for God alone.

Philo comes closer. In *De ebrietate,* 86, he points out that the wise man, when he retires far from human habitation, "serves Being alone." In *De praemiis et poenis,* 24, he urges the reader to be "pleasing to the Creator and Father of all things (alone), despising the things which the crowds admire, glory, riches, pleasure." He promises as reward "the vision of God" (27), the ability to "rejoice in God, the Father and Creator of all things" (32), and even good health (119), earthly blessings, and at the end, immortality (110). The combination of Greek philosophy and Hebrew faith is particularly manifest in Philo. Yet in spite of similarities, Philo's vocabulary is quite different and cannot represent the matrix from which the text in Mt derives.

The same is true of Greek and Latin philosophers whose writings touch on the importance of practicing virtue in secret, such as Seneca, Letter XIX,4(113),32, "He who wants his virtue to become known, acts not for virtue, but for glory," or Epictetus, *Diatribai* III,12,16f, where he suggests an ascetic practice and adds, "then tell no one," in order to preserve purity of intention. The concern here is not so much to please God alone as it is to exercise one's autonomy, and these texts have only a tangential bearing on the passage in Matthew.

A number of rabbinic texts contain the idea of serving God in secret, such as *Sotah* 9a, "She does it in secret, but he who sits in the secret place, the Most High, looks upon her";[27] *Sifre* 35a, "It is said that the Egyptians 'sinned secretly, and God made them known publicly.' If as regards the Attribute of Punishment, which is small, he who acts in secret is made known by God publicly, how much more, in regard to the Attribute of Goodness, which is great (will God make known deeds of goodness done secretly)";[28] *Shulchan Aruch,*

27. Cited by W.C. Allen, *A Critical and Exegetical Commentary on the Gospel according to St. Matthew*[3] (Edinburgh: Clark, 1912) 57.

28. C.G. Montefiore, *Rabbinic Literature and the Gospel Teachings* (London: Macmillan, 1930) 112.

"He who fasts, and makes a display of himself to others, to boast of his fasting, is punished for this";[29] *Mechilta to Ex* 19:2, "You call in secret, but I will answer you publicly."[30] Other passages, especially commentaries on Prov 21:14, are cited by Strack-Billerbeck.[31]

How are these texts to be evaluated? Do they express the thought of the rabbis (Pharisees) in the time of Jesus? They were written down several centuries after the death of Jesus, but they were meant to fix oral traditions that had been handed down equally for centuries. Do they represent a background of Mt 6:2ff, a reform movement of which the call for purity of intention in Matthew would be a part? Exegetes tend to think so. Eduard Schweizer, for instance, in his commentary on Mt 6:2 which urges the reader not to sound his horn when giving alms as the hypocrites do, writes: ". . . the saying (6:2) does not propose anything more than a reform, one which might have been possible even within Judaism."[32] This is perhaps the best way to express it: contact with rabbinic literature cannot be denied, but since we know so little about the historical circumstances underlying that literature, especially at the time of Jesus, we can only postulate the possibility of a reform within Judaism which criticized worldy motivation in the practice of almsgiving, prayer, and fasting along the lines of Mt 6:2–6,16–18.

4. Reward (negative: 6:2d,5d,16d; positive: 6:4b,6c,18b).

One of the first striking characteristics of this section is the exactness of repetition. The Amen-saying is repeated in exactly the same way each time, even at the cost of introducing the only second person plural into 6:2–4, and the corresponding saying about "thy Father who sees in secret" is repeated exactly, with only one word change, *kruphaiō* in 18b for its synonym *kruptō* in vv.4b and 6c. The threefold repetition is an essential part of the structure, uniting the sayings on almsgiving, prayer, and fasting into a compact, easy-to-

29. *Ibid.,* 138.

30. Schlatter, *Matthäus,* 203.

31. H.L. Strack and P. Billerbeck, *Kommentar zum Neuen Testament aus Talmud und Midrasch* I (Munich: Beck, 1922) 391f, 402.

32. Schweizer, *Matthew,* 143.

memorize text. The antithetical sayings on reward make the essential point very clear. They are a conclusion to the respective negative and positive teaching.

"They have received their reward"

In Koine Greek the verb *apechō* was used in receipts and implied that one had received his due and was entitled to nothing else. *Apechousin,* the form used in Mt 6:2,5,16, is present in form but aorist in meaning.[33] A. Deissmann published a list of ostraca which served as receipts between 300 B.C. and 63 A.D., all with the verb *apechō,* "I have received."[34] The verb is used in this sense also by Josephus (*Wars* I,596) and twice in the Septuagint: Gen 43:23 and Num 32:19. The term was so common that the Greek noun *apochē,* "receipt," became a Hebrew loan-word, *appôkî,* as in *Sifre Deut.* 26: *kātab lô appôkî,* "he wrote him a receipt."[35] In Mt 6:2,5,16 we have an ironic use of commercial language in a religious context. Those who act in order to be seen *are* seen; that is their reward, and they will get no other.

"Thy Father who sees in secret will reward thee" (6:4b,6c,18b)

Israel always believed that God was just, that he rewarded the good and punished the wicked, but the manner in which this was done seemed mysterious and complex. In the early centuries the group idea prevailed, and God could reward and punish collectively. In the time of Jeremiah and Ezekiel individual responsibility was stressed (Jer 31:29f; Ez 14:12–20; 18:1–32), and the problem of retribution was treated accordingly: each one according to his deeds, in this life. Belief in reward or punishment after death is not clearly expressed before 2 Mac 7:9–36, although the Book of Job grapples mightily with the problem, expresses a daring hope in 19:25–27, but ends with the silence of 40:2–5 and the humility of 42:2–6. Similar

·

33. J.H. Moulton and G. Milligan, *The Vocabulary of the Greek Testament* (London: Hodder & Stoughton, 1930) 57.

34. A. Deissman, *Licht vom Osten*[4] (Tübingen: Mohr, 1923) 88–90.

35. Cited by Schlatter, *Matthäus,* 202.

approaches to a belief in reward after death for fidelity to the Lord are found in some of the Psalms, especially Ps 73:24; 49:15f, and in some biblical apocalyptic texts such as Is 26:19 and Dan 12:1–3, but these are sporadic utterances, and the general Old Testament faith was a firm belief in the justice of God without trying to specify how or when he carried it out, though the normal presumption was that it would be in this world.[35a]

This same trust in the justice of God is manifested in rabbinic literature, including the fundamental Old Testament conviction that the reward and punishment would take place in this life.[36] The rabbis further developed the theme that God would requite "measure for measure," and numerous parables, stories, and sayings exist to prove that specific actions have precise consequences, good or bad, collectively or personally. Some rabbinic texts speak of reward and punishment in the hereafter, but they are few and were interpreted to include a this-wordly dimension as well. Thus for instance the statement "know that the giving of the reward to the righteous is in the time to come" was interpreted by R. Tarfon in such a way as to make the reward in this world precede that in the world to come.[37] The same attitude was expressed by the saying, "These are the things whose fruits a man enjoys in this world, while the capital is laid up for him in the world to come."[38] Such a faith made it of course difficult to explain the suffering of the righteous in this world, and the only answer one could ultimately give was that of the Book of Job.

The New Testament, by contrast, emphasized very much the concept of reward in the life to come, at the time of eschatological fulfillment. The verb *apodidōmi* is used in Mt 6:4,6,18 to express the idea of reward, and is normally translated "he will reward" (RSV;JB;NEB). Surprisingly, this verb with the meaning of "re-

---

35a. Cf. G.W. Nickelsburg, Jr., *Resurrection, Immortality, and Eternal Life in Intertestamental Judaism* (Cambridge: Harvard University Press, 1972), for the origin of the concept of reward in life after death as vindications of the unjustly oppressed slightly before the great persecution of Antiochus Epiphanes IV (175-164/3 B.C.). It then had a fairly extensive development in extra-biblical apocalyptic literature.

36. E.E. Urbach, "Reward and Punishment," *The Sages. Their Concepts and Beliefs,* 2 vols. (vol. 2 contains the notes to vol. 1; Jerusalem: Magnes Press, 1975) 436–444.

37. Cited by Urbach, 437.

38. *Ibid.,* 441.

ward" or "repay" on the part of God for man's good works is not found in Mk or Lk, or elsewhere in Mt except in the more general sense of "requite," Mt 16:27. This points once again to the uniqueness of expression in Mt 6:2–6,16–18.

The New Testament shares with the Old and with rabbinic Judaism the concept of reward for virtue and punishment for vice. It even shares with at least parts of the later Old Testament and with certain movements within early Judaism an eschatological outlook, that the reward (or punishment) would take place at the end-time, when the Son of man will come with his angels in the glory of the Father (Mt 16:27). This is expressed also in Mt 6 by the future tense, "(thy Father) *will* reward thee," *apodōsei,* and by the contrast with the hypocrites who already "have received," *apechousin,* their reward. It is the kingdom prepared for the just from the foundation of the world (Mt 25:34), that is, eternal life (25:46). Even the expression "treasure in heaven" (Mt 6:20/Lk 12:33; Mk 10:21 par) pertains to the eschatological way of thinking, so that it is not the reward of the individual in heaven after he dies, but rather his participation in the final glory when it comes. That reward will be great, in fact, "exceedingly great": Mt 5:12/Lk 6:23; also Lk 6:35. The exceeding generosity of God can be seen by his willingness to cancel debts of 10,000 talents (Mt 18:24,27). There is no proportion between the good deed done and the reward received; even a cup of cold water given in true charity will be rewarded (Mt 10:42).

There are several notes of distinction between the Hebraic and New Testament concepts of divine reward. The most fundamental is the idea of gratuity. The disciple of Jesus was a slave, not a hireling, and as such had no right to a reward: Lk 17:7–10. But as a slave he belonged to the household, and if he still received a reward, it was not strictly due to him, he did not "earn" it, it was a gift. And the gift was precisely a more intimate union with the Master, a closer collaboration. This is shown especially in the parables of the slaves waiting for the Master to come home from the wedding feast (Mt 24:46f/Lk 12:43f): the faithful servant is put in charge of all the Master's possessions; cf. the parable of the talents, Mt 25:14–30; Lk 19:11–27. This closer union is expressed also in Mt 6:4,6,18: "thy Father who sees in secret will reward thee" for acting before his divine gaze alone. This implies a relationship so intimate that not even the left hand knows what the right is doing: only the Father knows, and he will reward.

Another distinctive characteristic of the New Testament teaching on divine reward is its de-emphasis on reward in this life which was so typical of the Old Testament, especially in the Book of Deuteronomy, and which was maintained by the rabbis. A correlative is the refusal to regard earthly misfortune as punishment. This is expressed clearly in the story of the man born blind (Jn 9:3), but is found already in the Synoptics, e.g. Lk 13:1–5. The Christians experienced suffering and persecution just as Jesus did, even to the point of martyrdom; their reward for fidelity would come later, in the eschatological end-time.

The Greco-Roman idea of reward for virtue followed a different path.[39] The playwrights and historians showed that evil was punished in this life, by blindness (Iliad 2,599f), madness (Herodotus VI,75–84), lightning (Euripides, Phoen 1172–1186), etc., and that goodness was equally rewarded in this life, by prosperity (Odyssey 19,109–114). The philosophers, however, beginning with Socrates and Plato, taught that it would be unworthy of a virtuous man to be good for the sake of a reward, either from men or from the gods; virtue ought to be performed for its own sake. Thus in the *Republic,* II,366e, Plato pointed out that justice is practiced "by its own inherent force," that it is within the soul, and that it escapes the eyes of both the gods and men. He believed of course in immortality, and felt that a good life would continue as such even beyond death, and an evil life would be punished "tenfold" even after death (*Republic* X,615ab). Aristotle did not concern himself with reward after death; he limited his vision to this world, and saw in reason and man's desire for happiness the driving force of an ethical life (*Nicomachean Ethics* 1099b–1100a). Epictetus spoke of the all-pervading presence of God who sees what men do (*Diss* I,3,1ff; 6,40; etc.). He also emphasized that happiness was to be found in the virtuous life. Seneca, in *De vita beata,* 9,4, said: (virtus) *ipsa pretium sui!* Hellenistic and mithraic cults, on the other hand, did express the concept of divine reward for virtue.[40]

39. On the concept of reward in the Greco-Roman world cf. *TDNT* IV, 703–706.

40. *Ibid.,* 704f.

CONCLUSION OF THE SECTION ON TRADITION

Our analysis has shown the many original features of this text, its sapiential character, its tight unity, and its acceptance of fasting as a religious practice side by side with almsgiving and prayer, without emphasizing any of these three. Indeed, the exact similarity of treatment of all three is surprising. The central point is the purity of intention, done for God alone, an intimate Father who will surely reward. Woe to the hypocrites who seek earthly praise: they shall get nothing more. The intellectual climate which this text mirrors is early Judeo-Christianity. The practices mentioned are basic to Judaism; the hypocritical actions take place at the street corners and in the synagogues, but the hypocrites are not named Pharisees; a reward is promised. Yet the text also manifests some of the typical characteristics of Jesus' preaching: the closeness of the Father, the necessity of seeking him alone, the laying bare of hypocrisy and its total rejection, the linking of the future reward to the Person of the Father, and, by implication, to the time of eschatological fulfillment.

LEVEL OF REDACTION

Now that we have studied Mt 6:2–4,5f,16–18 as a unit in itself, prior to its insertion into the Gospel according to Matthew, we must see how it fits into that Gospel. It is part of the Sermon on the Mount, chapters 5–7, and so we shall try to determine its place in that structure.

Mt 6:2–18 is introduced by 6:1, composed by the final redactor, using vocabulary from 6:2–6,16–18, but adding a new concept, *dikaiosunē 'umōn,* "your piety" (RSV). *Dikaiosunē* is used seven times in Mt, never in Mk, and only once in Lk. The expression *dikaiosunē 'umōn* appears in the Synoptics only in Mt 5:20 and 6:1, and there is a close connection between the two texts. Mt 5:20 is part of the introductory paragraph 5:17–20 which is then followed by the six antitheses of vv 21–48; 6:1 is a second introductory statement followed by the three examples of vv 2–18. These are the two main blocks of material in the central section of the Sermon on the Mount, and are followed by a third, 6:19—7:12. The expression "the Law and the Prophets" appears in both 5:17 and 7:12, thus forming an inclusion.

The two introductions, 5:17–20 and 6:1, provide an answer as to how the material that follows is to be understood. 5:17–20[41] is a complex unit which centers on three themes: (a) the "Law and the Prophets"; (b) fulfillment by Jesus; (c) the need to exceed the righteousness (*dikaiosunē*) of the "scribes and Pharisees" in order to enter the kingdom of heaven.

The "Law and the Prophets" which Jesus came "not to abolish but to fulfill" (5:17) is the written Old Testament seen from two distinct points of view, as the normative expression of the will of God which remains valid somehow for all time,[42] and as a prophetic preparation for something yet to come.[43] Its fulfillment by Jesus is likewise a twofold reality. He fulfills it both as law and as prophecy: as law, by putting it into practice,[44] at least as regards its essential expression of the will of the Father which Jesus reasserts and explains in the antitheses, vv 21–48, and as prophecy, because his activity and teaching were the term towards which the Old Testament had been directed.[45] The relationship of the two verbs in 5:17, "abolish"—"fulfill," is to be seen not as contradictory but as relative, "superlative," as Wellhausen suggested.[46] "Fulfill" then means "bring to full reality," "deepen." Thus the Old Testament ceases to some extent, insofar as it was a prophecy which is now fulfilled in Jesus, but it continues in another respect, in a new and higher way as law.

The need to exceed the "righteousness"of the scribes and Pharisees (5:20) then relates to the deepening of the Law by Jesus in his activity and preaching. *Dikaiosunē 'umōn* refers to the total religious existence of man, like the *sᵉdāqā* of the Old Testament, fidelity to the Law; it is the carrying out of the will of God. Since it is now taught by Jesus in a new and deeper way, one's living it must also be more profound. The six antitheses which follow 5:17–20 then illustrate the new profundity of the Law.

---

41. The bibliography on these four verses is vast. See W. Trilling, *Das Wahre Israel*³ (Munich: Kösel-Verlag, 1964) 167–186; J. Dupont, *Les Béatitudes* I (Louvain: Nauwelaerts, 1958) 130–145; III (Paris: Gabalda, 1973) 245–266.

42. Mt 7:12; 22:40.

43. Mt 11:13.

44. Mt 3:15.

45. Trilling, *Das Wahre Israel,* 177; Dupont, *Béatitudes* I, 141.

46. Cited by Trilling, 178.

6:1 puts the practices of almsgiving, prayer, and fasting under that same category, *dikaiosunē 'umōn,* and demands by implication that same superiority over the scribes and Pharisees in performing these religious acts. The reference to scribes and Pharisees in 6:1 can be seen by the unique relationship of the expression *pros to theath-ēnai autois,* "to be seen by men" of 6:1 with that same expression in 23:5, denouncing the scribes and Pharisees (23:2); these are the only two instances of the expression in the New Testament. The "hypocrites" of 6:2,5,16 also become the "scribes and Pharisees, hypocrites" of 23:13,15,23,25,27,29. We are now in the context of the Judeo-Christian Church of 80 A.D., the time of the final redaction of Matthew, with its awareness of being distinct from Judaism. The Old Law is abrogated insofar as it prepared the coming of Jesus, but insofar as it expresses God's perennial will, it still remains, in a new and higher way. The practices of almsgiving, prayer, and fasting are also still valid, but they too must be renewed, by being performed exclusively for the Father who sees in secret.

Joachim Jeremias points out an important characteristic of the Sermon on the Mount in general.[47] It is a teaching, a "didache," an early Christian catechism. Perhaps it formed part of the instruction of catechumens, of those about to be baptized, or of those just baptized. It reflects a Jewish background, and so the disciples in question would have been converts from Judaism. They had to learn how their new life differed from the old, and although the Sermon on the Mount is not a complete statement of the Christian faith, it nevertheless gives the spirit of it very well, and touches on many essential points. Its power is especially apparent if we realize what preceded it, namely the "kerygma," the proclamation of the good news of salvation through Jesus Christ. They had heard that Jesus was the Messiah, that he died for the forgiveness of their sins, that he was raised on the third day, all in accordance with the Scriptures (1 Cor 15:3–5, the oldest text of the kerygma), and that he would come again. In him they were freed from the bonds of Satan and sin, and they now belonged to his heavenly kingdom. They had found the pearl of great price, they themselves were the guests at the wedding banquet. Now

47. J. Jeremias, *The Sermon on the Mount.* The Ethel M. Wood Lecture at the University of London, March 1961 (London: Athlone Press, 1961).

they had to learn how to be worthy of that great calling. The Sermon on the Mount taught them that, and it included, among other things, instructions on the right way to fast.

LEVEL OF THE HISTORICAL JESUS

Although a number of authors feel skeptical about our ability to arrive at Jesus as the source of the sayings in Mt 6:2–6,16–18,[48] or are unsure,[49] others feel that we can do so.[50] I think these latter authors present convincing arguments in favor of hearing at least the voice of Jesus behind the pericope, even though we cannot expect the Matthean text to give us his *ipsissima verba*. It should also be pointed out that Matthew attributes these sayings to Jesus, and that they should be accepted as such unless there is convincing proof to the contrary.

In many ways the teaching of Mt 6:2–6,16–18 on almsgiving, prayer, and fasting is not new. The prophets had already urged their hearers to have concern for the poor (Am 2:6–8; Is 3:14f), true religion of the heart (Am 5:21–24; Hos 6:6; Mi 6:6–8), and sincerity in fasting (Is 58:1–12; Jl 2:12f). Even the promise of a reward has a long history in Judaism. This should not surprise us, nor should it be taken as an argument that therefore Jesus could not have made these pronouncements. They simply show that Jesus was a man of his time, and that he spoke to the people in a language they understood. And, in fact, there is something new, a radical violence that goes beyond the admonishments of the prophets. Jesus called for a total forgetfulness of self: not to let the left hand know what the right was doing; to shut the door behind you in the closet as you pray; to anoint your head and wash your face while fasting, the very things forbidden on the Day of Atonement! Only someone free from the narrow traditions of the Jewish leaders could have said these things, someone passionately concerned about unique and total service to

---

48. Betz, "Eine judenchristliche Kult-Didache," 456f; Davies, *Setting of the Sermon on the Mount,* 307–315.

49. Gerhardsson, *The Testing of God's Son,* 76; Bultmann, *History of the Synoptic Tradition,* 133, n.1.

50. Bornkamm, *Jesus of Nazareth,* 84f; W. Grundmann, *Das Evangelium nach Matthäus*[4] (Berlin: Evangelische Verlagsanstalt, 1975) 190; George, "La justice à faire dans le secret," 597f.

the Father, someone willing to carry his cross and urging his disciples to do so. Anything less was a waste of time, a forfeiting of one's true reward from the Father. And though the total forgetfulness of human acknowledgment is difficult, Jesus demands that it be done with joyful abandonment, as a child absolutely sure of being seen and rewarded by a loving father. Here the pericope on fasting gives us the best clue that it comes ultimately from Jesus, for washing and anointing were signs of joy, preparations for a feast, and a festive spirit in the midst of difficulty is quite characteristic of Jesus. The Beatitudes already show signs of it: Blessed are you poor; blessed are you that hunger now; blessed are you that weep now (Lk 6:20f). He who finds the treasure hidden in a field "joyfully goes and sells all he has" (Mt 13:44); Zacchaeus received Jesus "joyfully" (Lk 19:6) and was willing to repay fourfold; Jesus proclaimed the joy of generous service, which was an echo of his own joy in total sacrifice, the complete giving of self on the cross, and of his own certainty of being known and loved by the Father (Mt 11:25–27).

A final point has yet to be considered—the tension between Mt 6:16–18 and Mk 2:18–22 par, from which it appears that Jesus abrogated fasting. This will be treated more fully in a future chapter. Here it is sufficient to note that tensions can exist without being contradictory, as for example between Jesus' call to "go into your room and shut the door" when praying (Mt 6:6) and yet to "let your light so shine before men that they may see your good works" (Mt 5:16). What is at stake is an inner attitude. One does not pray to let others see how well one prays; one prays totally for God, for him alone; others will then be encouraged by this good example and will praise God for it. Mt 6:16–18 does not say how often one should fast. It simply says "when you fast," and gives the rule of total dedication to "thy Father who is in secret."

CONCLUSION

As Jesus proclaimed the coming of the kingdom and called all to repentance during a period of about three years, he undoubtedly touched on many aspects of religious life in Palestine, including fasting. His main concern was the inner spirit with which it was to be performed, with purity of intention, as a sign of worship in loving submission to one's heavenly Father, and not as a means of gaining the approval of others. He also promised a reward in the coming kingdom.

The Palestinian Church which tried to put the teaching of Jesus into some kind of order then formed the didactic text basically as we find it today in Mt 6:2–6,16–18. It became part of a larger complex, the Sermon on the Mount, as an early Christian catechism. The spirit of pure intention which Jesus had demanded was to be a characteristic of Christian fasting which distinguished it from its Judaean counterpart. Finally, in the Gospel according to Matthew, it became part of Jesus' inaugural discourse, stating as completely as possible his program of the new kingdom.

The traditional practice of fasting, along with almsgiving and prayer, thus retained its importance as an act of worship.

Excursus

The Glosses on "Prayer and Fasting" (Mt 17:21; Mk 9:29; Acts 10:30; 1 Cor 7:5)

According to almost unanimous consent among text critics since Tischendorf, including Kurt Aland and the scholars at Münster (1975),[51] the words *kai nēsteia,* "and fasting," were added to *proseuchē,* "prayer," in Mt 17:21; Mk 9:29; 1 Cor 7:5, and a similar addition of "fasting" to "praying" occurred in Acts 10:30.

The expressions in Acts, "worshiping the Lord and fasting" (13:2), "fasting and praying" (13:3), "prayer and fasting" (14:23), together with the relationship between prayer and fasting in Mt 6, doubtlessly paved the way for the entrance of the above glosses into the text of the Bible. According to P[50] Cornelius is presented as "praying and fasting" (Acts 10:30) prior to the unexpected events that led to his baptism; the addition of *nēsteuōn* in 10:30 reflects the early Church's practice of fasting before being baptized (Did 7,4: "You shall order the one to be baptized to fast one or two days before"). The addition of *kai nēsteia* in Mk 9:29 may date back to P[45]

---

51. K. Aland *et al., The Greek New Testament*[3] (United Bible Societies, 1975) 66,159,456,591.

(3d c.); the papyrus is torn after the word *proseuchē*, but the spacing of the other words leads the specialists to conclude that *kai nēsteia* was written on the part torn off: Aland uses the symbol P[45]vid. P.L. Couchard argued not only that *kai nēsteia* was written in the missing space, but also that it was the original reading of Mk 9:29.[52] Quoting Strack-Billerbeck I,760, he pointed out that fasting normally accompanied the exorcism of demons.

The addition of "fasting" to "prayer" in all the above texts shows the great emphasis placed by the Church on fasting as a means of strengthening prayer. It is something it learned from the Old Testament (Ezr 8:21–23; Neh 1:4; 9:1ff; Est 4:16; 2 Mac 13:12; Sir 34:26), maintained during its early formation (Acts 13:2f; 14:23), and continued to stress, especially in the third and fourth centuries.

Conclusion

Although Mt 17:21 and Mk 9:29 cannot be invoked as Synoptic texts which treat of fasting as a means of strengthening prayer, for *nēsteia* is a later gloss, the glosses themselves attest to the validity of the concept, which is, indeed, expressed elsewhere in both the Old and New Testament.

---

52. P.L. Couchard, "Notes sur le texte de St. Marc dans le Codex Chester Beatty," *JTS* 35 (1934) 3–22. Most authors rightly disagree. If the expression "and fasting" had been part of the original reading of Mk 9:29, why would the MSS S* B it[k] geo[1] Clement have omitted it? The correct explanation is given by B.M. Metzger, *A Textual Commentary on the Greek New Testament* (United Bible Societies, 1971) 101: "In light of the increasing stress in the early church on the necessity of fasting, it is understandable that *kai nēstei*a ("and fasting") is a gloss which found its way into most witnesses."

CHAPTER SIX

The Pharisee and
the Tax Collector
(Lk 18:9-14)

Although the mention of the semi-weekly fast of the Pharisee in Lk 18:12 has no parallel in the other Synoptic Gospels, it does manifest a certain kinship of spirit with the criticism of the fast of the hypocrites in Mt 6:16–18. Similarly, just as the Matthean passage speaks of a reward, the Lucan text takes up the matter of justification. We will seek to come to a fuller understanding of the teaching about fasting (and prayer) contained in these verses of Luke by considering them from the threefold level of redaction, tradition, and history.

TRADITION

It is generally pointed out that the text on the Pharisee and the tax collector is one of the most semitic of Luke's Gospel, a strong indication that Luke received the account from tradition.[1] V.14b is found with slight variation in Lk 14:11 and Mt 23:12, which indicates that it was an independent saying of Jesus put here as a commentary on vv 10–14a; v 9 is an introduction to the parable which may have been added prior to Luke, but which may also stem from Luke himself.[2]

---

1. J. Jeremias, *The Parables of Jesus*[3] (London: SCM Press, 1972) 139–142.

2. See M.E. Boismard's notes to P. Benoit *Synopse des Quatre Evangiles en français* II (Paris: Du Cerf, 1972) 305, where he cites several statistics in favor of the Lucan redaction of 18:9.

The literary genre of vv 10–14a is an "exemplary story," closely related to the parable but without the figurative elements of the latter; it presents a model to be followed. J. Jeremias contents himself with Luke's designation, *parabolē* (18:9);[3] Louise Schottroff discusses both terms and prefers the expression "exemplary story" because it centers attention on the reaction of the hearer, which is the most significant aspect of this type of account.[4] Other examples are Lk 10:29–37, the Good Samaritan (v 37: ". . . go and do likewise"); 12:16–21, the Rich Fool; and 16:19–31, the Rich Man and Lazarus.

A more difficult question is the degree of historical accuracy contained in the presentation of the two figures. We all know that the Pharisee is the villain and the tax collector the hero, but how is this indicated, and at what point in the story? J. Jeremias presumes that the hearer did not know this until the very end. He cites 14a and adds:

> Such a conclusion must have come as a complete surprise to its hearers. It was beyond the capacity of any of them to imagine. What fault had the Pharisee committed, and what had the publican done by way of reparation?[5]

Louise Schottroff shows convincingly that such is not the case. The reader (or hearer) knows long before 14a that the Pharisee is the one whose conduct is blamed and the tax collector the one who is praised. She demonstrates from the literary character of the account itself that the Pharisee is presented as a caricature right from the start, and the tax collector as an "identification figure."[6] The purpose of such descriptive elements as "standing" and "with himself" is not to indicate precisely what happened, but rather to show that there is something strange about this person. That reaction—intended by these words—is immediately confirmed by the content of the Pharisee's "prayer": "not like the rest of men" (*all* men; no exceptions are

3. Jeremias, *Parables,* 139,142.
4. L. Schottroff, "Die Erzählung vom Pharisäer und Zöllner als Beispiel für die theologische Kunst des Ueberredens," *Neues Testament und christliche Existenz,* Festschrift for H. Braun, ed. by H.D. Betz (Tübingen: Mohr, 1973) 439–461, esp. 444.
5. Jeremias, *Parables,* 144.
6. Schottroff, "Die Erzählung vom Pharisäer und Zöllner," 448–454.

made!), "robbers, swindlers, adulterers." No one prays like that! This is not a prayer at all; it is a caricature of a prayer. The tax collector, by way of contrast, is portrayed in such a way as to allow the hearer to identify with his humility. Every Jew could pray with him, "O God, be merciful to me, a sinner," all the more so since the first words come from the beginning of Ps 51. The modesty and humility of the tax collector are exaggerated just as is the self-righteousness and pride of the Pharisee, in order to win sympathy for him.

The further description of the Pharisee's "prayer" is a recital of certain acts of piety that probably stood out in the minds of people as especially typical of the Pharisaic movement, but in an exaggerated way. The "good Pharisee" is depicted as one who fasts twice a week and gives tithes on everything he buys, just as a "good Catholic" is sometimes ironically described as one who refrains from eating meat on Friday and goes to Mass on Sunday. There is an element of truth in the description, but also of exaggeration, and of condemnation. The Catholic is condemned in the very portrayal for considering this to be the essence of religion, while forgetting much more important things such as love of neighbor; the Pharisee is condemned for his self-righteousness and contempt for others.

Verse 14a gives the verdict: "Believe me, this man went home from the temple justified but the other did not" (New American Bible). J. Blank notes that the background to v 14a is to be found in the cultic *zaddiq*-sentence of the priests which presumably accompanied certain liturgical ceremonies at the gate of the Temple.[7] Those who were declared "just" were allowed to enter the Temple and worship there. Remnants of such a *Toraliturgie* are Ez 18:5–9, Ps 15:1–5; 24:3–6; Is 33:14–16.[8] The tax collector is judged to be in correct relationship with God. He humbled himself and begged pardon for his sins. One is reminded of Ps 51:19: "The sacrifice acceptable to God is a broken spirit; a broken and contrite heart, O God, thou wilt not despise."

What conclusion may be drawn about the value of fasting twice

---

7. J. Blank, *Schriftauslegung in Theorie und Praxis* (Munich: Kösel-Verlag, 1969) 151.

8. W. Zimmerli, *Ezechiel* (Neukirchen-Vluyn: Neukirchener Verlag, 1969) 397–400.

a week? That it is worthless if done in a spirit of self-righteousness and disdain for others. We return here to the criticism of the prophets, both about fasting, Jl 2:12–14; Is 58:12, and about offering sacrifice, Am 5:21–27; Hos 6:6–8; Is 1:11–17: it is the heart, the inner spirit with which it is done, that counts.

REDACTION

V 14b, probably not part of the original story, is a good generalization and commentary on God's judgment of the Pharisee and the tax collector: "everyone who exalts himself will be humbled, but he who humbles himself will be exalted." Though it cannot be shown that Luke was the first to add this independent logion of Jesus to vv 10–14a, it nevertheless fits very well with his basic point of view. It may even be said that Luke considers the whole of God's salvific activity in Jesus to be the humbling of the proud and the lifting up of the lowly: Lk 1:15, "He has put down the mighty from their thrones and exalted those of low degree"; 2:34, "Behold, this child is set for the fall and rising of many in Israel"; 3:5f (Is 40:4f), "Every valley shall be filled, and every mountain and hill shall be brought low . . . for all flesh shall see the salvation of God"; 14:11, as part of vv 7–14, on choosing the last place; 16:15; 16:19–31, the Rich Man and Lazarus; 19:7.[9]

The introductory sentence v 9 is likely to be Lucan; it too expresses the fundamental conviction of Luke that it is not "those who trust in themselves that they are righteous and despise others" who will be saved, but rather those who acknowledge their need of mercy. By leaving the expression vague, "those who . . .", Luke allows us to examine our own conscience and see whether or not we ourselves might be meant, and to repent before it is too late. At the same time Luke assures us that we *can* be saved, that no one is beyond the pale of God's mercy, if only we repent. He is the only evangelist who preserves for us the account of the justification of the tax collector instead of the Pharisee (18:9–14), the forgiveness of the sinful woman

9. R. Glöckner, *Die Verkündigung des Heils beim Evangelisten Lukas* (Mainz: Matthias-Grünewald Verlag, 1975) 135–138.

in the presence of Simon who despised her in his heart (7:36–50), the salvation of Zacchaeus who was "lost" while the crowd looked on and murmured (19:1–10), and the picture of the repentant prodigal son and his brother who refused to go in and rejoice (15:11–32). While Luke did not create these stories, he nevertheless used them effectively, both to exemplify God's loving mercy and salvation, a fundamental theme of his Gospel, and to warn the reader against hardness of heart, for which the penalty is condemnation. Applying this to fasting, we could say that Luke cautions the reader to be humble and not proud in his/her special act of virtue, and not to look down on others who do not fast, for salvation is denied to "those who trust in themselves that they are righteous and despise others," while it is freely granted to the repentant sinner who begs for God's mercy. It would be too much to say that Luke is against fasting, for he presents Anna, the widow in the Temple, with obvious sympathy, and goes out of his way to point out that she worshiped "with fasting and prayer night and day" (2:37); he also kept Mk's statement "then they will fast" (Lk 5:35), and noted examples of fasting in Acts 9:9; 13:2–3; 14:23; 27:9, but he never emphasized it, as did Matthew, and in the figure of the Pharisee he let it be known that fasting can also be a source of pride and contempt for others.

HISTORICITY

We have already noted the semitic tone of the account. Its general content is typical of a Palestinian society in which the character and basic religious orientation of the Pharisees and tax collectors were well known. The reversal of socially accepted judgments, the condemnation of self-righteousness in the figure of the revered Pharisee and the commendation of humble repentance in that of the despised tax collector are in line with what we know of Jesus. His predilection for outcasts, and especially for tax collectors, can be seen in his choice of Levi as an apostle, and in the harsh accusation that he was a "glutton and a drunkard, a friend of tax collectors and sinners" (Q: Mt 11:19/Lk 7:34). There is no real reason to doubt the authenticity of this parable. As I. H. Marshall points out, ". . . the case that Jesus is unlikely to have used this story, or that the story would have been persuasive only in the situation of the Church, remains unconvincing."[10]

CONCLUSION

At the various levels of history, tradition, and redaction the judgment about the twice-weekly fast of the Pharisee remains surprisingly constant: it is to no avail, because of his inner attitude of self-righteousness and contempt for others. The very one who ought to have been—and was generally considered to be—a model of virtue was shown to be sadly deficient, his acts of external piety vitiated by pride and hatred, while the one whose profession made him synonymous with "sinner" was justified because he begged for God's mercy. As an "exemplary story," Lk 18:9–14 teaches us that we too can receive God's mercy, even if we are as sinful as a tax collector, but only if we humbly ask for it, and it warns us not to vaunt ourselves for our good works or look down upon others who may not be as pious, for otherwise our inner sin will cancel everything and we will be condemned. If Crossan is right in positing an initial "parable,"[11] then perhaps there is the added dimension of God's grace, the arrival of the kingdom of God which turns accepted values upside down, challenging the hearer to accept the unthinkable, that Samaritans, tax collectors, and the poor can be "good" and saved!

10. I.H. Marshall, *The Gospel of Luke* (Exeter: Paternoster Press, 1978) 678.

11. J.D. Crossan, "Parable and Example in the Teaching of Jesus," *NTS* 18 (1971/72) 299f.

CHAPTER SEVEN

The Question About Fasting
(Mk 2:18-22 par)

One of the most interesting and important New Testament texts on fasting is the powerful and intriguing answer of Jesus to those who accused his disciples of not fasting: "Can the wedding guests fast while the bridegroom is with them? As long as they have the bridegroom with them, they cannot fast. The days will come, when the bridegroom is taken away from them, and then they will fast in that day" (Mk 2:19f). Many questions come to mind. Does this mean that Jesus and his disciples did not fast? Was there any special significance to his self-designation as bridegroom? Does the text reflect a mood of joy that is infectious and that makes us want to be part of the group surrounding Jesus? Can such a spirit of joy still be maintained today? Has he been truly "taken away" or does he still remain? How are we to interpret the saying, "then they will fast in that day"?

There are three accounts of the same scene: Mt 9:14-17; Mk 2:18-22; Lk 5:33-39. Do they represent three different traditions or do they derive from a single source? If so, from which one? What part did the early Christian community have in the formation of these texts? Do they accurately reflect the words of Jesus?

An initial answer to these questions is supplied by the Two-Source theory on the relationship of the Synoptic Gospels to each other, namely that Matthew and Luke independently used the Gospel of Mark as a source, along with Q.

The Two-Source Theory

The three accounts of the question about fasting are very similar; they have the same development of thought and sometimes exactly the same vocabulary, especially Mt 9:15b/Mk 2:20/Lk 5:35 and Mt 9:17/Mk 2:22/Lk 5:37f. There are also a number of differences of detail, and several minor agreements between Mt and Lk against Mk. The occurrence of such close similarity with minor variation in detail points to literary, rather than oral, dependence. Several theories have been proposed to explain the relationship of these accounts, but the classical Two-Source Theory is still the best. It is the simplest; it explains satisfactorily both similarity and variation without multiplying sources. We therefore presuppose the priority of Mk, and consider that both Mt and Lk used his account in their own redactions, and independently of each other made such changes in the text of Mk as they deemed necessary, either for reasons of style, for the cumbersome, repetitious, non-literary rendering of Mk left much to be desired, or in order to express more emphatically their own theological concerns.[1]

Tradition and the Historical Jesus

Mt 9:14–17 and Lk 5:33–39 have no outside information on the question of fasting which does not come from Mk 2:18–22. In trying to arrive at the level of tradition, then, we must begin with the text of Mk. It is widely acknowledged that Mk 2:18–22 is itself part of a pre-Marcan collection of controversies (2:1—3:6), the second of two related pericopes that deal with Jewish-Christian differences on eating with "sinners" and fasting; it is followed by another double series on sabbath observance, 2:23 and 3:1–6.[2]

---

1. This theory is rightly held by many commentators. The case is argued well by A. Jülicher, *Die Gleichnisreden Jesu* II (Tübingen: Mohr, 1910) 178–202, and a good summary can be found in F.G. Cremer, *Die Fastenansage Jesu* (Bonn: Peter Hanstein, 1965) 1–4.

2. Signs of pre-Marcan compositions: 3:6 comes too early in the plan of Mark; the use of a further conflict-story in 3:22–26 (Beelzebul) is strange after 3:6; the allusion to Jesus' death in 2:20 does not harmonize with 8:31; cf. V. Taylor, *The Gospel according to St. Mark*² (London: Macmillan, 1966) 91f.

The controversy about fasting is actually limited to vv 18–20, for 21f are a parabolic addition on the incompatibility of old and new, and were put here as a commentary on the fasting dispute.

In describing the literary genre of 18–20, and its *Sitz im Leben,* two levels must be distinguished. As the verses stand now, they constitute a "controversy" and follow the basic pattern of that genre:

1. short portrayal of the controversial situation, though incomplete, v 18a;
2. criticism by the opponents, here in interrogative form, v 18b;
3. answer of Jesus, vv 19–20.

But if we begin with v.19a, we become aware of the presence of another genre, which Bultmann called *Apophthegm* and Vincent Taylor termed a "Pronouncement-Story," in which the saying is central, but there is a short narrative leading up to that saying. The close connection between these genres is seen by the very fact that Bultmann placed "controversy" as a sub-heading under the general category *Apophthegms.*[3]

Let us begin by studying the individual elements of the "controversy" as given above.

1. Short Portrayal of the Controversial Situation (Mk 2:18a)

"Now John's disciples and the Pharisees were fasting; and people came and said to him" (2:18a).

Both Mt and Lk omitted the notice of Mk that the "disciples of John and the Pharisees" were fasting, for it stands in tension with the question that follows. The ones who pose the question are indeterminate: *kai erchontai kai legousin autō:* "And people came and said to him . . ." (Revised Standard Version; cf. the similar translations in the New American Bible, the New English Bible, the Chicago Bible, etc). The introduction mentions "the Pharisees" while the following question speaks of the "disciples of the Pharisees." V.18a was there-

---

3. R. Bultmann, *The History of the Synoptic Tradition* (Oxford: Blackwell, 1972) 18f.

fore not part of the original account, and is redactional, either of Mk, or of the pre-Marcan complex. The introduction was limited originally to "And people came and said to him . . ." and the controversial situation was implicit in the question.

2. Criticism by the Opponents (Mk 2:18b)

"Why do John's disciples and the disciples of the Pharisees fast, but your disciples do not fast?" (2:18b)

Although it is not clear who actually poses the question, the contrast is between the "disciples of John and the disciples of the Pharisees" who fast, and the disciples of Jesus, who do not fast. John was noted for his severity as regards food (Mk 1:6, "eating locusts and wild honey"; Mt 11:18/Lk 7:33 = Q, "neither eating nor drinking") and it is quite understandable that his disciples would have fasted too. The precise motive of their fast is not stated, but it was probably akin to the spirit of the Ninevites who fasted in repentance on hearing the preaching of Jonah (Jon 3:5); it would have been their participation in the repentance preached and practiced by John (Mk 1:4).[4] Perhaps it was even an "eschatological demonstration" of their preparation for the final age.[5] The Pharisees too were known for their fasting: Lk 18:12; Did 8:1; Strack-Billerbeck IV,77–114.[6] Did their "disciples" also fast? It is generally pointed out that the Pharisees as such did not have disciples, only those Pharisees who were also scribes.[7] This leads us to conclude that the mention of the "disciples of the Pharisees" is a redactional element intended to intensify the conflict, and was probably formed on the pattern of the "disciples of John" and the disciples of Jesus. Originally, before the account became part of the "controversy" series 2:1—3:6, the difference of attitude toward fasting was limited to that between the

4. Ch. H.H. Scobie, *John the Baptist* (London/Phila.: SCM/Fortress, 1964) 139ff.

5. J. Becker, *Johannes der Täufer und Jesus von Nazareth* (Neukirchen-Vluyn: Neukirchener Verlag, 1972) 26.

6. See above, chapter 2.

7. H. Schürmann, *Das Lukasevangelium* (Freiburg: Herder, 1969) 294; A. Feuillet, "La controverse sur le jeûne (Mc 2,18–20; Mt 9,14–15; Lc 5,33–35)," *NRT* 90 (1968) 126.

disciples of John and those of Jesus.[8] Some exegetes have argued in favor of the originality of the expression "disciples of the Pharisees" as being the *lectio difficilior*,[9] but the basis on which this opinion is grounded, namely Mt 22:16 and Mt 12:27/Lk 11:19, is too small and ambiguous; at best it can be considered a later usage that refers simply to the "adherents" of the Pharisaic way of life.[10]

The grouping of the disciples of John with the disciples of the Pharisees is artificial, all the more so since in Mk 3:6, the end of this section, the former are no longer mentioned. The only thing they have in common is that they both fast, in contrast to the disciples of Jesus, who do not fast. It is an allusion to this fact, and nothing more. Anyone who knew of this contrast could have posed the question, and indeed we are not told who did ask it. But it was an interesting question: why did the disciples of Jesus not fast?

3. Answer of Jesus (Mk 2:19-20)

"And Jesus said to them, Can the wedding guests fast while the bridegroom is with them? As long as they have the bridegroom with them they cannot fast. The days will come when the bridegroom is taken away from them, and then they will fast in that day" (2:19-20).

The answer is even more interesting, for it has all the earmarks of an authentic word of Jesus, at least 19a: "Can the wedding guests fast while the bridegroom is with them?" The semitic tone of the answer is assured by the expression "the sons of the bridechamber," a literal translation of *bnê haḥuppāh;* here it means "wedding guests" in general.[11]

Jesus answered the question with a question, according to rabbinic fashion, and used images drawn from daily life. The answer is obviously "no," not "while the bridegroom is with them." Whatever

8. Feuillet, 126; Jülicher, *Die Gleichnisreden Jesu,* 179; J. O'Hara, "Christian Fasting. Mk 2:18–22," *Scripture* 19 (1967) 87.

9. TDNT IV,443; C.E.B. Cranfield, *The Gospel according to St.Mark*[2] (Cambridge: University Press, 1963) 108.

10. Feuillet, "La Controverse sur le jeûne," 126; Schürmann, *Lukasevangelium,* 294.

11. *TDNT* IV, 1103, n.40; Taylor, *Mark,* 210.

the deeper overtones of this expression, it is in any case a profound one. It shows that the non-fasting of the disciples of Jesus was not simply due to laxity or lack of piety or even to a negative judgment on fasting as such; it was rather a positive sign of the joyous arrival of the long-awaited messianic age. Since ancient times wedding imagery was associated with eschatological fulfillment (Is 61:10; 62:5); this is developed especially in a number of New Testament parables (Mt 22:2–14; 25:1–12[13]) and metaphors (Jn 3:29f), as well as in rabbinic literature (e.g. Ex Rabba 15,79b, ". . . the wedding will take place in the days of the Messiah").[12] Jesus wanted to emphasize the spirit of the final age being inaugurated by him, and that is why his disciples were not known for their fasting.

Did the answer of Jesus limit itself to a generic expression of messianic wedding joy, or did it also identify the bridegroom as himself? Several points must be made. First of all, it is quite possible that the expression "while the bridegroom is with them" simply means "while the wedding is going on."[13] Also, there is no certain proof that "bridegroom" was ever used as a title of the Messiah in the Old Testament and early rabbinic Judaism. This was shown by Joachim Jeremias in *TDNT* IV,1101f and has been generally accepted.[14] W.H. Brownlee, in "Messianic Motifs in Qumran and the New Testament," *NTS* 3(1956/57) 12–30,195–210, tried to show that there was some evidence in IQ Is^a (61:10) of "bridegroom" as a late Jewish messianic title, but J. Gnilka, "Bräutigam—spätjüdisches Messiasprädikat?" *TrThZ* 69 (1960) 298–301, demonstrated that Brownlee's arguments were quite weak. Since then, however, J. Jeremias did discover an example of bridegroom/Messiah in rabbinic literature, Pesiq.149a, but it is a late text; Jeremias concludes: "This isolated and very late example does not affect the general picture."[15]

---

12. *TDNT* IV, 1102; Strack-Billerbeck I,517f; G. Minette de Tillesse, *Le secret messianique dans l'Evangile de Marc* (Paris: Du Cerf, 1968) 124f.

13. *TDNT* IV, 1103; Jülicher, *Die Gleichnisreden Jesu,* 186.

14. O'Hara "Christian Fasting," 93f; Minette de Tillesse, *Le secret messianique,* 124f; other authors, however, feel that on the basis of Ps 45 there were some messianic overtones to the word "bridegroom": Feuillet, "La controverse sur le jeûne," 133f; Taylor, *Mark,* 210f.

15. J. Jeremias, *The Parables of Jesus*[3] (London: SCM, 1972) 52, n.12.

Another aspect to be considered is that in the Old Testament Yahweh was the bridegroom and Israel the bride (Hos 1–3; Ez 16:7ff; 23:4; Is 50:1; 54:4ff), which would mean that if Jesus did apply the term to himself it would have had connotations of being divine, and exegetes hesitate to ascribe such a self-determination.[16] It is not necessary, however, to be so explicit, and it is quite possible that Jesus simply wanted to indicate his coming as the inauguration of the eschatological age characterized by the joy of a wedding without entering into exact detail as to who and what the bridegroom was. But one thing seems to be sure: he used the refusal to fast like the disciples of John and the Pharisees as a sign that the start of the Messianic age had finally arrived.[17] At the same time he would have given indirect witness to himself, for the people would certainly have wondered who the bridegroom was.[18] At the level of tradition it was certainly the crucified and risen Lord, but even during his lifetime there was a veiled reference to himself as the bringer of that salvation. If we take the expression "while the bridegroom is with them" as a hint that Jesus would not always be with his disciples,[19] then perhaps we can go further and conclude that the non-fasting of the disciples is justified not by the Messianic age as such, but by the presence of Jesus as its inaugurator. Here we run into the problem of allegory. Jülicher[20] may have overstated his case, and perhaps we are not forced to choose between two extremes, no allegorical identification of the bridegroom or guests on the one hand, and an explicit Messianic or divine declaration on the other, attributing the former to Jesus and the latter to the Church. I think it is possible to see in the actions

16. Not all; see Feuillet, "La controverse sur le jeûne," 134; Minette de Tillesse, *Le secret messianique,* 125.

17. O'Hara, "Christian Fasting," 93f, who justly quotes J.M. Robinson, *A New Quest of the Historical Jesus* (London: SCM, 1966) 22: "Between the false alternatives of 'just general truths' or 'explicit claim to messianic titles' there lies in Jesus' public ministry a whole area of eschatological action accompanied by theological commentary."

18. Schürmann, *Lukasevangelium,* 296.

19. W.G. Kümmel, *Promise and Fulfillment* (London: SCM, 1961) 76f; R. Pesch, *Das Markusevangelium* (Freiburg: Herder, 1976) I, 173; J. Roloff, *Das Kerygma und der irdische Jesus* (Göttingen: Vandenhoeck & Ruprecht, 1970) 233.

20. Jülicher, *Die Gleichnisreden Jesu,* 186–188.

(non-fasting) and images (bridegroom, guests) used by Jesus a certain implicit identification. This does not mean that the problem of non-fasting/fasting is reduced to a matter of dates, or that Jesus wanted to legislate later fasting practice in any way. I also hope to show in the following section that vv 19b.20 are a later addition. But even in 19a there is a certain emphasis on feasting because of the presence of Jesus, the initiator of the Messianic age, who would not always be present.[21]

The answer of Jesus is twofold; in v 19a he justified the nonfasting of the disciples (this is repeated in slightly different form in 19b, as a preparation for 20), and in v 20 he announced the future return to fasting of the early Church. We have argued for the authenticity of the first part (19a). Is the second (19b.20) also a word of the historical Jesus?

The stated reason excusing from fasting is the presence of the bridegroom "with them" (*met' autōn*), and the justification for its resumption "on that day" is his absence "from them" (*ap' autōn*). Note that the *met autōn* of 19a is repeated in 19b, precisely as a contrast to the *ap'autōn* of 20. In the first part the identification with Jesus is only hinted at; in the second it is unmistakably presupposed.[22] In the first part the point of view is from that of the bridegroom (while "he is" [*estin*] with them); in the second, it is from that of the disciples (while "they have" [*echousin*] him with them, 19b; when he shall be taken away from them, 20). There is also a shift of emphasis from the *en 'ǭ*, "while," of 19a to *'oson chronon*, "as long as," of 19b. The formulation of 19b is from a time when the non-

---

21. R. Pesch, *Das Markusevangelium,* 173; Feuillet, "La controverse sur le jeune," 262; Roloff, *Das Kerygma und der irdische Jesus,* 226f; H. Patsch, *Abendmahl und historischer Jesus* (Stuttgart: Calwer Verlag, 1972) 199, is very careful: he considers v.19a an authentic word of Jesus, but does not think it intends to say anything about an intermediate period after his death, nor does he allow us to accept the figure of the bridegroom as a veiled self-designation of Jesus, but he does grant a christological component to the saying, namely, that "it is Jesus himself who announces authoritatively the presence of the kingdom, not only in general terms, but in connection with himself and with the relationships established thereby." This was then taken a step further by the community and allegorized to mean Jesus = bridegroom.

22. R. Pesch, *Das Markusevangelium,* 171; Roloff, *Das Kerygma und der irdische Jesus,* 230.

fasting of the disciples of Jesus was already considered an exception: "as long as they have the bridegroom with them."[23]

I believe Jesus did reckon with an interval between his death and the final eschatological consummation,[24] but I do not feel that he wanted to regulate the practice of fasting after his death, or that in answer to criticism he would have specified that non-fasting was valid only during his lifetime. He probably said something short, simple, and cryptic like v 19a. The rest is easily explainable as an addition by someone in the early Church, putting the answer of Jesus in line with later practice.

Several authors, especially K. Th. Schäfer and F.G. Cremer,[25] deny that the Church would have created vv 19b.20 to justify the renewed acceptance of fasting, for the early Church Fathers did not cite Mk 2:20 in this connection. The primitive Church simply took over the Jewish practice of fasting two days a week, changing the days from Monday and Thursday to Wednesday and Friday (Did. 8,1), without citing any word of the Lord in apology. They further emphasize that vv 19b.20 are authentic, but do not refer to fasting in the literal sense, at least primarily. The main point is that the disciples will mourn once the bridegroom is "taken away."[26] There is much valuable Church history in these works, especially those of Cremer, and they must be taken into account, although it is perhaps not necessary to arrive at the same conclusions. I think the problem has been formulated incorrectly. Authors frequently state that vv 19b.20 were added in order to justify the Church's renewed acceptance of fasting. That is phrasing the problem wrongly. The Church did not need any justification for its practice, for it was part and parcel of the religious culture of the time, as is shown clearly in the Di-

23. Among the many authors who consider Mk 2:19b,20 a later addition: Schürmann, *Lukasevangelium,* 297; Pesch, *Markusevangelium,* 174; Roloff, *Das Kerygma und der irdische Jesus,* 233; Bultmann, *History of the Synoptic Tradition,* 18f.

24. Kümmel, *Promise and Fulfillment,* 77, and passim; Patsch, *Abendmahl und historischer Jesus,* 123,126,129; Feuillet, 265.

25. K. Th. Schäfer, ". . . und dann werden sie fasten," *Synoptische Studien,* Festschrift for A. Wikenhauser, ed. by J. Schmid and A. Vögtle (Munich: Karl Zink Verlag, 1953) 124–147; F.G. Cremer, *Die Fastenansage Jesu.*

26. Schäfer, 141; Cremer, 5f; Feuillet, 261.

dache, and as the writings of Schäfer and Cremer have rightly emphasized. The problem was something else, namely the de-emphasis on fasting by Jesus and his disciples, to the point of arousing the criticism of being a glutton and a drunkard (Mt 11:19). And so vv 19b.20 were added, not to justify the Church's later attitude, but rather to put the anomalous contrary practice of the disciples of Jesus, as manifested by Mk 2:19a, into perspective: as an exception during the public ministry of Jesus. If one asks: Why did the Church hand on Mk 2:19a? then one can answer with Schürmann, because it was furnished with vv 19b.20.[27] Both aspects are important, the exception in the public ministry of Jesus to emphasize that the new age had begun in his person, and the ordinary rule, fasting as a continued sign of worship here on earth.

Jesus was of course not against fasting, if done in the right spirit (Mt 6:16–18), and he doubtlessly fasted on the Day of Atonement in accordance with Jewish law, but he wanted to emphasize the special eschatological nature of his coming, and he expressed it in a variety of ways, including the non-fasting of his disciples. Also, he considered it more important to be in intimate table companionship with outcasts and sinners, to make them aware of the Father's forgiveness and grace, than to have fidelity to various practices of tradition.

A final hint that vv 19b.20 would have been added later is the manuscript addition of "and fasting" to certain passages on prayer (Mt 17:21; Mk 9:29; 1 Cor 7:5; Acts 10:30); this shows that there was a tendency in the Church to add an emphasis on fasting that was not found in the original text.

We have tried to show that the verb in the expression "and then they will fast on that day" of v 20 is to be taken literally, and that it refers to the period after the "taking away" of the "bridegroom," that is, after the death of Jesus. But what is the meaning of the final phrase, "on that day"? To what does "that day" refer? The phrase "on that day" is already redundant after "then" and is in contrast with the beginning of the verse, "days will come." Matthew omitted "on that day" completely, which is all the more surprising since he copied the rest of Mk 2:20 exactly, word for word; Luke changed it to the plural, to agree with the "days" of the first part. In Mk we

27. Schürmann, *Lukasevangelium*, 297.

have three indications of future time: "Days will come ... then ... on that day." If "on that day" were simply to mean "at that time," it would add nothing new to "then," and we would have a tautology; to say that it "adds a peculiar impressiveness to the forecast"[28] is scarcely a satisfactory explanation.

H.J. Ebeling[29] tried to prove that the "bridegroom" would be "taken away" at the time of the Messianic woes and that the Church would fast then, but Kümmel[30] pointed out that the concept of an absent Messiah at the time of the Messianic woes is not found in late Judaism or primitive Christianity. Georg Braumann[31] suggested that "on that day" be taken as a technical term for the Last Day, in connection with Last Judgment and the eschatological woes, but that is an indirect return to the unacceptable opinion of H.J. Ebeling, and has been rejected.[32] And so we are left with the meaning of "on that day" as referring to a particular day. H. W. Kuhn[33] has classified the varying opinions of exegetes as to which day is meant into four groups: 1. Friday of each week; 2. the Paschal fast of the Quartodecimans; 3. Holy Saturday; 4. Good Friday.

Good Friday and Holy Saturday cannot be the days meant by Mk's "on that day," for in the first century the annual celebration of Easter on a Sunday was not yet introduced, nor the annual celebration of Good Friday or Holy Saturday.[34] The Paschal Fast of the Quartodecimans is also ruled out as very improbable, for their purpose in fasting was originally vicarious atonement for Israel, and not in memory of the death of Jesus, nor did they fast on the anniversary day of his death.[35] The most probable allusion of Mk 2:20 is to a weekly fast on Friday. The Jews fasted two days a week, Monday

28. Taylor, *Mark,* 211.

29. H.J. Ebeling, "Die Fastenfrage (Mk 2.18–22)," *Theologische Studien und Kritiken* 108 (1937/38) 387–396.

30. Kümmel, *Promise and Fulfillment,* 75f.

31. G. Braumann, " 'An jenem Tag' Mk 2,20," *NT* 6 (1963) 264–267.

32. Pesch, *Markusevangelium,* 175, n.22; Roloff, *Das Kerygma und der irdische Jesus,* 232, n.101.

33. H.W. Kuhn, *Aeltere Sammlungen im Markusevangelium* (Göttingen: Vandenhoeck & Ruprecht, 1971) 66–72.

34. For the arguments, see Kuhn, 68, n.94; B. Lohse, art. "Ostern," *RGG*³ IV, 1735f; W. Huber, *Passa und Ostern* (Berlin: Töpelmann, 1969) 45ff.

35, Kuhn, *Aeltere Sammlungen im Markusevangelium,* 68, notes 92 and 93; *TDNT* V, 902.

and Thursday. They chose these days as a matter of convenience, that is, in order not to fast on the sabbath, and to have as wide a space between the two fasts as possible. From the *Didache* 8,1 a first-century text, we know that the Christians rejected fasting on Monday and Thursday, but chose to fast instead on Wednesday and Friday. Cremer points out that no word of the Lord was cited for the change of days, and in fact no specific reason is given.[36] Why did the early Christians pick these days? Because the sabbath was changed from Saturday to Sunday? Probably, but why did they not choose Tuesday and Friday as a logical alternative to Monday and Thursday? Cremer's explanation that the Christians probably followed the calendar of Qumran and the Book of Jubilees, and that in this calendar Wednesdays and Fridays are important liturgically, does not satisfy. Yes, these days were important, Wednesday as the day on which the world was created, and Friday as the day before the sabbath, but that does not mean these should be Christian fast days. The most logical explanation is that the Christians fasted on Friday in honor of the death of Jesus. This is the "day" referred to in Mk 2:20. The Jews however fasted twice a week, and the Christians wanted another day, so they chose Wednesday, partly in order to have a second day of fasting, and also because of its connection with the Passion. This is still the best hypothesis and the one held by most exegetes.[37]

The Parabolic Sayings (Mk 2:21f)

"No one sews a piece of unshrunk cloth on an old garment; if he does, the patch tears away from it, the new from the old, and a worse tear is made. And no one puts new wine into old wineskins; if he does, the wine will burst the skins, and the wine is lost, and so are the skins; but new wine is for fresh skins" (Mk 2:21f).

These sapiential observations about the incompatibility of new and old were originally independent sayings of Jesus[38] put here by

---

36. Cremer, *Die Fastenansage Jesu,* 11.

37. H.W. Kuhn, *Aeltere Sammlungen im Markusevangelium,* 69f, holds this opinion, and cites the following: A. Loisy, Bacon, Dibelius, Lohmeyer, Hirsch, Behm, Klostermann, Burkill, Bowman, Schweizer, and Haenchen.

38. Pesch, *Markusevangelium,* 177; A.E.J. Rawlinson, *The Gospel according to St. Mark* (London: Methuen, 1925) 32: "We do not know—and it is idle to guess—in

the pre-Marcan editor as a commentary on the question about fasting, now part of the dispute 2:1—3:6. If 2:18-22 is at the center of this section, as seems likely,[39] then it is most probably because of this distinction between new and old.

As far as fasting is concerned, these sayings imply that the fasting of Christians should somehow be different from that of the Jews. In its present context, that would indicate a new meaning to the fast, and a different time of fasting.

REDACTION

In Mark, the question about fasting, 2:18-22, is the center of the controversy section 2:1—3:6 which ends with the decision of the Pharisees and Herodians to join forces against Jesus, but which emphasizes, especially for the reader, the new liberation brought about

what context they were originally spoken. They are characteristic sayings of Jesus, unforgettable in their homely vividness and power."

There are two *logia* in the Gospel of Thomas which are directly connected with Mk 2:18-22, *logion* 104, related to vv. 18-20, the question about fasting ("when the bridegroom comes out of the bridechamber, then let them fast and pray"), and *logion* 47, which includes the images of vv 21f, that is, a patch on a garment (there: *old* patch on *new* garment), new wine old wineskins (and old wine in new wineskins), and also a version of Lk 5:39 ("no one drinks old wine and immediately desires to drink new wine"). Although G. Quispel in "The Gospel of Thomas and the New Testament," *Vig Chr* 11(1957):189–207, esp.192–195, tried to demonstrate that these *logia* derive from an independent tradition, probably an Aramaic Gospel of the Hebrews, it is still more probable that they derive from the Synoptic Gospels themselves, as R. McL. Wilson, *Studies in the Gospel of Thomas* (London: Mowbray, 1960), 77–79, 84f, R.M. Grant, "Notes on the Gospel of Thomas," *Vig Chr* 13(1959):170–180, esp. 176f, H. Schürmann, "Das Thomasevangelium und das lukanische Sondergut," *BZ* 7(1963):236–260, esp. 238–240 (=*Traditionsgeschichtliche Untersuchungen zu den synoptischen Evangelien*, Düsseldorf: Patmos-Verlag, 1968, pp. 228–247, esp.230f), and W. Schrage, *Das Verhältnis des Thomas-Evangeliums zur synoptischen Tradition und zu den koptischen Evangelienübersetzungen*, BZNW 29 (Berlin: Töpelmann, 1964), 112–115, have shown. On *logion* 47 cf. also F. Hahn, "Die Bildworte vom neuen Flicken und vom jungen Wein (Mk 2,21f par), "*EvTh* 31 (1971) 365–367.

39. J. Dewey, "The Literary Structure of the Controversy Stories in Mark 2:1–3:6," *JBL* 92 (1973) 394–401.

by him: forgiveness of sins, healing, friendship with tax collectors and "sinners," presence of the bridegroom, fasting determined in relation to him, freedom from unrealistic sabbath restrictions. It is an age of new wine, and people must become new wineskins. There is a sense of freshness and exhilaration in this ancient statement of faith. At the center is Jesus, the Messiah, inaugurator of the long-awaited eschatological age. Jesus was acknowledged as the one in whose presence we experience the joy of a wedding, which even the allusions to the Passion, as in 1:14 and 3:6, do not dampen. The examples of liberation were unassailable and continued to be important for the early Christians. There was a clear promise of divine presence (2:7,19) and demand for renewal. Fasting too benefited from this new climate, for it now brings about a closer awareness of the Person of Jesus. At the same time it was given second place; its transitory, commemorative character was acknowledged: at the fullness of Messianic plenitude there will be no fasting, just as there was not for the brief, festive appearance of the bridegroom.

Matthew took over all of Mk 2:1—3:6 but he separated it into two parts, with the healing of the paralytic, the call of Levi and the question of fasting as one unit (9:1–17) and the plucking of grain and the healing of the woman with the withered hand, both on the sabbath, as another (12:1–14). The first unit is part of a larger whole, namely the ten miracle stories of Mt 8–9, which immediately follow the Sermon on the Mount, Mt 5—7, and which together constitute a twofold section on Jesus as the Messiah in word (5–7) and deed (8–9), set off by an inclusion, 4:23 and 9:35.

Matthew joined the question about fasting more closely to the presence of Jesus and his disciples at a dinner given in his honor by the newly-called Levi, to which tax collectors and "sinners"[40] were also invited. Instead of the anonymous questioners of Mk, here the disciples of John the Baptist come up and ask; in his answer, Jesus begins by using the verb "mourn" (*penthein*) rather than "fast," and he uses the expression *eph' 'oson*, "as long as," rather than the more neutral *en 'ọ̄*, "while," of Mk, in order to give greater emphasis to the future absence of the bridegroom, understood as Jesus himself, and

---

40. *TDNT* I, 328: those who do not follow the Pharisaic ordinances.

to mourning as the Church's reaction: "Can the wedding guests mourn as long as the bridegroom is with them?"

It is sometimes pointed out that the Aramaic word *'it'annê* underlies both the text of Mt and Mk, and that it was translated by *nēsteuein* in Mk 2:19 and *penthein* in Mt 9:15,[41] but this has also been denied by others.[42] While it may be theoretically possible, it is not likely. J. Dupont noted that in the LXX *penthein* is never used to translate the Hebrew *'anāh,* which is given in Greek mostly by the verb *tapeinoō* (fifty-three times, not counting Sir).[43] There is of course a close connection between the two ideas, for one of the signs of mourning is fasting (1 Sam 31:13; 2 Sam 1:12; 3:35). By changing the first verb to "mourn" and by eliminating "on that day" of Mk 2:20, Matthew emphasized the pain of separation that took place after the departure of Jesus from this life (and the joy of his presence while he was here). For Mt, the idea of mourning characterized better than that of fasting the Christian attitude of waiting for the second coming of Christ. This is confirmed by Mt's only other use of the verb *penthein*, in the second beatitude, 5:4: "Blessed are those who mourn *(penthontes)*, for they shall be comforted." With mourning there is also the pain of persecution, but deep within there is joy, as the final beatitude points out, 5:11f: "Blessed are you when men revile you and persecute you . . . on my account; rejoice and be glad, for your reward is great in heaven. . . ." There was a certain sense of sadness, mourning, and yearning at the thought of not yet being in final fulfillment, but there was also the joy of anticipation and the happy remembrance of its first beginning in the coming of the bridegroom.

Matthew's earlier statements about fasting, 4:1–4 and 6:16–18, stand in some sort of tension with 9:14–17 which he was not able to eliminate. In 4:1–4 Jesus fasted, and in 6:16–18 he gave instructions on the proper attitude to have while fasting, while in 9:14 it is stated that his disciples did not fast, an allegation which Jesus did not deny and which his statement indirectly bears out, for if wedding guests

41. *TDNT* IV, 1103, n.41.

42. H.W. Kuhn, *Enderwartung und gegenwärtiges Heil* (Göttingen: Vandenhoeck & Ruprecht, 1966) 198.

43. J. Dupont, *Les Béatitudes* III (Paris: Gabalda, 1973) 552, n.3.

cannot mourn, they certainly cannot fast. Thus even in Mt, which emphasizes fasting more than the other Gospels, it is ultimately seen as a relative spiritual practice, as we wait.

Luke also accepted all of Mk 2:1—3:6, but in contrast to Mt he kept it in one block, 5:17—6:11, as part of a slightly larger section, 5:1—6:11, the New Order in the Community, itself the beginning of a still larger unit, 5:1—9:50, Jesus' public activity in the whole land of the Jews (including Galilee but not limited to it), prior to the journey to Jerusalem, 9:51—19:27.

Even more than Matthew, Luke tied the question about fasting to the dinner at Levi's, but made it a contrast between "fasting often and offering prayers," on the one hand, and the disciples' "eating and drinking" (*esthiousin kai pinousin*), on the other, an allusion to both 5:30 and 7:34. By adding "often" Luke interpreted the fasting as an oft-repeated practice, similar to that of the Pharisee in 18:12, and by adding "offering prayers" he enlarged the question to include prayer, anticipating the sayings about new and old, and hinting that both fasting and prayer need to be distinguished from the similar practices in Judaism. Luke sharpened Mk's version of the answer of Jesus, "Can you make wedding guests fast . . .", but he kept the main point, not "while the bridegroom is with them," but "the days will come . . . and then they will fast." Mk had added "on that day"; Lk changed it to "in those days," referring to the whole time of the Church, for according to Acts 13:2f and 14:23 there was also a Christian fast, together with Christian prayer. Once again fasting revolves around the bridegroom: none in his presence, nor in the final consummation, Lk 22:16,18, but in the meantime, yes.

Lk's changes in Mk 2:21f also stress the new, and by using the idea of tearing a piece from a new garment in order to patch up an old one, he alludes to the danger facing the newly-formed Christian Church from a desire to return to the old, especially under pressure from certain Judaizers, and inculcates the need to develop a Christian praxis, distinct from that of Judaism. Lk 5:39 tries to explain why many have refused to join the Church, but it also contains the idea of the incompatibility between new and old, and might be an indirect warning to the community not to be attached to the old, which at times could seem to be more comfortable.

CONCLUSION

The image of the bridegroom is at the center of this question about fasting. The fact that the disciples of Jesus did not fast like those of John the Baptist or the Pharisees would not be so important were it not for the explanation given by Jesus in Mk 2:19a: "Can wedding guests fast while the bridegroom is with them?" Their non-fasting was intended to make a point, namely that the eschatological age had come in Jesus, and that in his presence one should rejoice, and not fast. It was a Christological act of faith and witness to Jesus.

The future return to fasting after his being "taken away" was therefore also related to Jesus, as a sad memorial of what happened on that fateful Friday, mixed with inner confidence and humble trust in his second coming and the final consummation of the parousia. This Christian fast was something new, distinct from that of Judaism, not only as regards the day of fasting, but more importantly, in terms of its inner motivation. Even as a sign of humble worship of the Father it was henceforth related to Jesus, through whom our salvation has come, and in whose presence we will one day rejoice without reservation, in the plenitude of his Kingdom.

CHAPTER EIGHT

A Glutton and a Drunkard
(Mt 11:16–19/Lk 7:31–35)

A comparison between Jesus and John, similar to that expressed in Mk. 2:18–20, is found also in Q, Mt 11:16–19/Lk 7:31–35, where the "Son of Man" is accused of being a "glutton and a drunkard, a friend of tax collectors and sinners," while John is described as one who came "neither eating nor drinking" (Mt) or "eating no bread and drinking no wine" (Lk). Our consideration of this passage will seek an answer to primarily two questions: What judgment is made about fasting—was Jesus really a glutton and a drunkard? And, in general, what was—according to the text—the relationship between Jesus and John on this point?[1] We will try to answer these questions at the threefold level of redaction, tradition, and history.

TRADITION AND HISTORY

The text consists of two sections, a parable (Mt 11:16f/Lk 7: 31f) and a saying (Mt 11:18f/Lk 7:33–35).

The parable is given in slightly different versions. Matthew presents two groups of children intending to play a game of weddings

---

1. The historical relationship between Jesus and John has been much discussed. From passages such as Lk 5:33; 11:1; Acts 19:3 it can be argued that the disciples of John the Baptist continued to exist as a separate group; at least some of the subordination of John to Jesus expressed in the New Testament seems to be an attempt by the early Church to call this group to order. Cf. G. Bornkamm, *Jesus of Nazareth* (New York: Harper & Row, 1960) 47f and notes 33–34: he feels that some Johannine disciples became Mandaean gnostics; J. H. Hughes, "John the Baptist: The Forerunner of God Himself," *NT* 14 (1972) 191–218. M. S. Enslin, "John and Jesus," *ZNW* 66 (1975) 1–18, denies that Jesus ever met John, but he gives no proof.

and funerals; as one group plays the flute, the other is supposed to do a wedding dance, and if the first ones wail, the second are to beat their breasts in mourning (*koptein*), but the second group refused to do either, and so the children quarreled, sat down in a market place, and the first accused the second (*tois 'eterois*). Luke seems to have imagined that as the first group piped, expecting the second to dance, the second one wailed, expecting the first to weep (*klaiein*), and the children sat down in the market place, quarreling and blaming one another (*allēlois*) for having ruined the game. The reason for the failure of the game in either case seems to be the same, namely the capricious stubbornness of the children. The men (Lk) of "this generation" (Mt/Lk) were compared to the children in general, because of their obstinacy, and the two games, wedding and funeral, seem to be an allusion to Jesus and John.[2]

The saying which follows contains several harsh judgments: John is accused of having a demon because of what is seen as his excessive asceticism, "neither eating nor drinking" (Mt), or perhaps "eating no bread (meat?) and drinking no wine" (Lk);[3] Jesus is rejected as being simply a glutton and a drunkard because of his open relationship with tax collectors and sinners.[4] These charges are not directly denied, but the credibility of those who make them is rejected, as seen by the pejorative use of "this generation," the link with

2. Cf. F. Mussner, "Der nicht erkannte Kairos (Mt 11,16–19/Lk 7, 31–35)," *Bib* 40 (1959) 599–612, esp. 600f.

3. Exegetes usually consider Lk's "bread" and "wine" an explanatory addition, or a gloss, possibly with a view to Lk 1:15. O. Böcher, on the contrary, in "Ass Johannes der Täufer kein Brot (Luk. vii.33)?" *NTS* 18 (1971) 90–92, feels that the longer Lucan version is primary, and that the "fasting" of John alluded to in Lk 7:33 is not a quantitative one but a qualitative one, the renunciation of meat (the original Aramaic *lᵉhēm* can mean bread, food, or meat) and wine, which were considered particularly demonic in antiquity. This would fit well with the notice that he ate locusts and wild honey (Mk 1:6/Mt 3:4), since locusts (and fish) were allowed to those who had vowed not to eat meat (M. Chullin 8, 1) and a drink made of honey substituted for wine. Jewish "fasting" can also mean renunciation of meat and wine: M. Ta'anit 4,7; bTa'anit 30b; bBaba Bathra 60b Bar; Tosefta Sota 15, 11–15.

4. On the expression "tax collectors and sinners" see J. Jeremias, *New Testament Theology* (London: SCM, 1971) 109–113; J. R. Donahue, "Tax Collectors and Sinners," *CBQ* 33 (1971):39–61, esp.57. W. Walker's opinion, in "Jesus and the Tax Collectors," *JBL* 97 (1978):221–238, that Jesus had no special relationship with the tax collectors and outcasts strikes me as completely without foundation. He certainly does not prove his contention.

the preceding parable, the harshness of the accusations, and the following sentence, that wisdom is justified by "all her children" (Lk), or by "her deeds" (Mt). The whole passage is in fact an accusation against *them* for not having recognized the meaning of the action of John as an ascetical sign of repentance, and the joy of the Messianic invitation of the Son of Man who shares the table with the outcasts of Israel's society, bringing them the eschatological joy of a wedding. Those who turn the activity of John and Jesus into an evil caricature are thereby accused of not having seen the signs of the times, final repentance, and the breaking in of the eschaton.

What historical situation best explains the text of Q? The following points can be made:

The parable (Mt 11:16f/Lk 7:31f) is semitic in tone, reflects a Palestinian milieu, is old, and can probably be attributed to Jesus himself, especially since there is a slight discrepancy with the interpretation that follows, vv 18f. The parable seems to have been originally independent; the saying was added later.

In the saying about the Son of Man (Mt 11:18f/Lk 7:33–35) the expression "a glutton and a drunkard" (*phagos kai oinopotēs*) is a traditional formula in Hebrew, using the present participles of the verbs *zālal*, to be a worthless glutton, and *sābā'*, to be a drinker: Dt 21:20—*zôlēl wᵉsōbē* (LXX: *sumbolokopōn oinophlugei);* Prov 23:21—*sōbē' wᵉzōlēl* (LXX: *methusos kai pornokopos);* Prov 23:20—*sōb'ê-yāyin, zōlᵃlê basar* (LXX: *oinopotēs ektinōn sumbolais kreōn agorasmois).* Note how fixed the Hebrew expressions are, and how fluid their LXX translations. This shows quite clearly the semitic coloring of the taunt. Note too that the rebellious son of Dt 21:20, "a glutton and a drunkard," was to be stoned to death (21:21). The traditional use of this expression, joined with "friend of tax collectors and sinners," shows well what the "sin" of Jesus really was: not at all gluttony and drunkenness, but his free mixing with Jewish social outcasts, his willingness to eat with those very ones whom the scribes and Pharisees shunned. This attitude of Jesus is frequently mentioned (Mk 2:15–17 par; Mt 21:31f; Lk 15:1f; 19:2–10), and each time we see its double aspect: the wonderful offer of God's eschatological nearness to those who least expect it, and the grim anger of the Jewish authorities. That this openness of Jesus is part of his mission, and not simply a natural attraction for tax collectors and sinners (without denying it, however), can be seen by such statements as "Those who are well have no need of a physician, but those who are sick; I came not to call the righteous, but sinners" (Mk 2:17); "the tax collectors and the harlots go into the kingdom of God before you" (Mt 21:31); "today salvation has come to this house" (Lk 19:9); and also in the passage under consideration, "Yet wisdom is justified by (all) her children" (Lk 7:35).

Such a widespread tradition about Jesus' special closeness to "tax collectors and sinners" is certainly based on historical fact. The sharpness of the taunt against Jesus in the present passage also argues for its historicity, for it is not the kind of saying that the early Church would have invented. The main problem about historicity is the presence of the expression "Son of Man" (Mt 11:19/Lk 7:34). Bultmann was willing to admit that an old saying could be the base of Mt 11:18f/Lk 7:33f, on condition that the "Son of Man" not have apocalyptic overtones but simply mean "man," as in Mk 2:10, 28; Mt 8:20 par."[5]

Although there is still much discussion about the origin of the title "Son of Man", there is a strong body of opinion that considers it to derive from the pre-Christian Jewish apocalyptic figure of Dan 7:13f which appears also in the Similitudes of Ethiopian Enoch and in IV Ezra, and which describes the Son of Man as being a pre-existent divine agent of judgment and salvation at the end of time.[6]

The title is used in three different contexts in the Synoptics, in "future" sayings such as Mk 8:38; 13:26; 14:62; Mt 10:32f/Lk 12:8f; Mt 24:27,37/Lk 17:24,26, where there is not always an identification between Jesus and the Son of Man, "suffering" sayings, found only in Mk, such as 8:31; 9:31; 10:33f, which are probably all redactional, and "present" sayings, such as Mk 2:10, 28; Mt 8:20/Lk 9:58.

Mt 11:19/Lk 7:34 belongs to this last group. R. H. Fuller "reluctantly" considers Mt 11:19 in its existing form as a "Church formation" but admits the possibility that an original "I" stood in place

5. R. Bultmann, *History of the Synoptic Tradition,* 165.
6. R. H. Fuller, *The Foundations of New Testament Christology* (New York: Scribner, 1965); J. Jeremias, *New Testament Theology,* 257ff; Bornkamm, *Jesus of Nazareth,* 175–178; B. Lindars, "Re-enter the Apocalyptic Son of Man," *NTS* 22 (1976) 52–72.

of the Son of Man;[7] J. Jeremias feels that Jesus did use the expression *bar ᵉnāšā,* with the indefinite meaning "one," which later became an apocalyptic title;[8] W. G. Kümmel agrees that Jesus used the expression in Mt 11:19, but meant it as a veiled allusion to his sovereignty.[9]

In the light of these differences, it would be hazardous to insist that Jesus used the term "Son of Man" in Mt 11:19/Lk 7:34, though we are on more solid ground if we accept the rest of the verse as authentic. In any case, as G. Bornkamm points out, even if Jesus did not apply the title to himself, he did speak about the coming Son of Man, judge of the world, in the sense intended by contemporary apocalyptic thought, and manifested an astonishing assurance that decisions made here and now about his person would be confirmed at the Last Judgment.[10]

We can conclude, then, that both traditions rest on reliable historical facts, namely that John did preach final repentance before the coming wrath of God, and that he practiced what he preached. Severity as regards food became known as a primary characteristic of him and his disciples. Jesus, on the other hand, was known especially for his willingness to associate with the outcasts of Israel's society in an effort to bring them the mercy and love of a new age. That is why the title "Son of Man" is appropriate in this context, for it has eschatological overtones and interprets the actions of Jesus in that light. The value of fasting as practiced by John lies in its being a preparation for that which was brought by Jesus. F. Mussner rightly calls this a "succession of periods in salvation history," first John, then Jesus.[11] This means that here too, as in Mk 2:18–20, fasting has a secondary place. It gives way to the wedding dance associated with Jesus. This is shown by the fact that John is mentioned first and Jesus second (Mt 11:18f par), though in the parable the dance was first, and the wailing second (Mt 11:17 par).

The joy brought by Jesus was however not permanent. His loving, open companionship with all was severely criticized. The Son of

---

7. Fuller, 125.
8. Jeremias, 266–268.
9. W. G. Kümmel, *Theology of the New Testament* (London: SCM, 1974) 44–46.
10. Bornkamm, 177.
11. Mussner, "Der nicht erkannte Kairos," 604.

Man was accused of being a glutton and a drunkard. If Jesus alluded to his death in Mk 2:19a, which was then made explicit by the Christian community in 19b,20, then a similar intuition is present here. The comparison with the stubborn children who refuse to play the game shows that same sad awareness of impending rejection that we found in Mk 2:19, and hints that the wedding joy brought by Jesus is only a brief inauguration and foreshadowing of that final one so long awaited and yet to come in its fullness. I would say further that the aura of joy is linked with the person of Jesus in Mt 11:16–19 par, just as it was in Mk 2:18–20. The Marcan text said that it would cease with his death, "and then they will fast"; Q does not go that far, but does point out that "this generation" dismissed Jesus with an uncomplimentary epithet, which, at least in Dt 21:20f, was associated with the rebellious son who was to be stoned to death.

REDACTION OF MT AND LK

Mt 11:16–19/Lk 7:31–35 was already part of a larger complex of Q prior to its incorporation into the Gospels. The text consisted most probably of Mt 11:2–11, 16–19/Lk 7:18f, 22–28, 31–35,[12] which portrayed John the Baptist as the Messianic forerunner of Jesus (cf. Mt 11:10/Lk 7:27), and Jesus himself as "the one who is to come," in whose works the prophecies of the Messianic age (Is 35:5; 29:18; 61:1) were being fulfilled (Mt 11:3–5/Lk 7:19–22). John's question about the Messianic nature of Jesus was meant not only for himself but for all Israel ("shall *we* look for another?"), including the men of "this generation," but they stubbornly refused to accept the true answer; instead, they rejected both John and Jesus.

Matthew seems to have made very few alterations in the underlying Q text of our pericope. If O. Böcher is correct in asserting that Lk's description of John as "eating no 'bread' and drinking no wine" (7:33) is original, and meant that John abstained from meat and wine like many other ascetics in antiquity,[13] then Matthew would have made a redactional change to show that John fasted, and this would be another indication of the Matthaean interest in fasting. He also

12. Mussner, 606.
13. Böcher, "Ass Johannes der Täufer kein Brot?" 90–92.

seems to have changed an original (Lk's) "children" to "works" in the final sentence. The text of Luke means that the wisdom of God in sending John and Jesus was "justified," vindicated by the adherence of the "children," the tax collectors and sinners, the outcast, while those in authority refused. Matthew, instead, says that the wisdom of God in sending John and Jesus was justified by the works which these emissaries performed, especially the works of Jesus referred to in 11:2.

Luke made many changes for the sake of style, but he expressed his theological concerns primarily by prefixing vv 29f to the text of Q, in order to avoid a possible misunderstanding about the "men of this generation" who rejected John and Jesus: it referred to the authorities only; "all the people," down to the tax collectors, "justified" God, as children of wisdom (v 35), by accepting his plan of salvation for Israel, now continued in the Church.

CONCLUSION

Our study of this text shows that the accusation against Jesus of being a glutton and a drunkard is without foundation, except for the free association with tax collectors and sinners, those who refused to follow the minute prescriptions of the Pharisees and who were therefore shunned by the latter. We saw further that the action of Jesus was a salvific one, bringing, as Son of Man, the Messianic joys of a wedding dance to all, even the outcasts. As such, this is in contrast with the figure of John, whose penitential severity with food made him seem like a mourner at a funeral, but he too "came" in the name of God, and though he was rejected along with Jesus by "this generation," the children of Wisdom accepted both his fasting and the joyous friendship of the Son of Man, and demonstrated thereby the validity of God's plan.

EXCURSUS:
THE SYNOPTIC FASTING ACCOUNTS:
PALESTINIAN OR HELLENISTIC?

In the preceding chapters I studied the Synoptic passages on fasting as carefully as possible in order to establish the relationship among the three levels of redaction, tradition, and history, and also in order to determine which of these texts pertain to the Palestinian Church and which to the Hellenistic. My conclusion is that all of them were either handed down or created (Mt 4:1–11/Lk 4:1–13; Mk 2:19b–20) by the Palestinian community. I found no indications of a Hellenistic origin or even Hellenistic coloring to the Synoptic texts on fasting. Also, in the rest of the New Testament fasting is hardly ever treated. Paul does not speak of it—1 Cor 4:11; 2 Cor 6:5; 11:27 refer not to fasting but to hunger as part of the hardships endured in his missionary activity;[14] John does not discuss it, nor do the Catholic epistles. Luke, in Acts, is the only one who mentions it. He states that Paul "neither ate nor drank" (9:9) for three days after his conversion experience on the way to Damascus, that the community of Antioch fasted and prayed before sending Paul and Barnabas off on their missionary journey (13:2f), and that the latter fasted and prayed (at Antioch?) before appointing elders in the churches (14:23). These are exceptions; the generalized picture Luke gives in Acts 2:46f hardly leaves room for fasting: "And day by day, attending the temple together and breaking bread in their homes, they partook of food with glad and generous hearts, praising God. . . ." One reason why fasting was not emphasized in the Hellenistic Church was the need to combat incipient gnosticism.[15] Col 2:20–23 is directed against those who say, "Do not handle, do not taste, do not touch";[16] 1 Tim 4:3 excoriates the "liars . . . who forbid marriage and

14. On 1 Cor 4:11 see C. Craig and J. Short, "The First Epistle to the Corinthians," *The Interpreter's Bible,* X (New York: Abingdon, 1953), 55f; H. Conzelmann, *I Corinthians,* tr. by J. Leitch (Philadelphia: Fortress Press, 1975), 89f. On 2 Cor 6:5 and 11:27 see F. Filson and J. Reid, "The Second Epistle to the Corinthians," *The Interpreter's Bible,* X, 347f, 402; R. Bultmann, *Der zweite Brief an die Korinther,* ed. by E. Dinkler (Göttingen: Vandenhoeck & Ruprecht, 1976), 172,218.

15. C. Spicq, "Hérétiques et hétérodoxes," *Les épitres pastorales,* I, 4th rev. ed. (Paris: Gabalda, 1969), 85–119; H. F. Weiss, "Paulus und die Häretiker. Zum Paulusverständnis in der Gnosis," *Christentum und Gnosis, BZNW* 37, ed. W. Eltester (Berlin: Töpelmann, 1969), 116–128; R.M. Grant, *Gnosticism and Early Christianity* (New York/London: Oxford University Press, 1959); H. von Campenhausen, *Die Askese im Urchristentum* (Tübingen: Mohr, 1949) = *Tradition und Leben,* Kräfte der Kirchengeschichte, Aufsätze und Vorträge (Tübingen: Mohr, 1960), 114–156; F. Amiot, *L'enseignement de Saint Paul,* Théologie Biblique, Série III, Vol. 7 (Paris: Desclée, 1967), 104–106; see also the three following notes.

16. H.F. Weiss, "Gnostische Motive und antignostische Polemik im Kolosser- und im Epheserbrief," *Gnosis und Neues Testament,* ed. by K.W. Tröger (Gütersloh:

enjoin abstinence from foods which God created to be received with thanksgiving";[17] even the suggestion to Timothy in 1 Tim 5:23 to "drink a little wine for the sake of your stomach and your frequent ailments" should be seen in this context.[18] We have already noted above that Greek ascetical movements, such as the Pythagoreans and mystery religions like Kybele, considered wine, meat, beans, and other food to be dangerously connected with demons and therefore urged abstinence from it. Not so the Pauline church.[19] Jesus had already declared all foods clean (Mk 7:18–23), the vision of Peter confirmed it (Acts 10:10–16), and 1 Tim 4:4 corroborated it: ". . . everything created by God is good." In general, the Hellenistic church did not emphasize fasting out of recognition that the new converts either did not have a tradition of fasting, or that their ideology of fasting was so interwoven with their pagan religion that in rejecting paganism totally it was better to omit fasting, though good in itself, lest there be brought with it concepts and attitudes of other aspects of paganism less in keeping with Christianity. It must not be thought that the Hellenistic church was morally lax. There was a real concern about temperance and self-control (Lk 21:34; Rom 13:13; 1 Cor 6:10; Gal 5:21; Eph 5:18; 1 Pet 4:3). Paul even said, "I pummel my body and subdue it" (1 Cor 9:27), and of course the on-coming persecutions demanded courage and fidelity in the face of torture and death.

Gerd Mohn, 1973),311–324; W. Hendriksen, *A Commentary on Colossians and Philemon* (London: The Banner of Truth Trust, 1971), 18–21,130–133; J.B. Lightfoot, "The Colossian Heresy," *Saint Paul's Epistles to the Colossians and to Philemon* (London: Macmillan, 1879), 73–113,202–208; Campenhausen, 131–133 (see previous note).

17. F. Gealy and M.P. Noyes, "I Timothy," *The Interpreter's Bible,* XI (New York: Abingdon, 1955), 425–428,445; S. de Lestapis, *L'énigme des Pastorals de Saint Paul* (Paris: Gabalda, 1976), 398; W. Hendriksen, *I & II Timothy and Titus* (London: The Banner of Truth Trust, 1960), 146–148; G. Haufe, "Gnostische Irrlehre und ihre Abwehr in den Pastoralbriefen," *Gnosis und Neues Testament,* 325–339 (see previous note); Spicq, 497–500.

18. C. Spicq, "I Timothée 5:23," *L'Evangile hier et aujourd'hui,* Mélanges offerts au Pr. F.J. Leenhardt (Genève: Labor et Fides, 1968), 143–150.

19. If Gal 4:10 includes the Day of Atonement or other fast days in its criticism of those who observe "days, months, seasons, and years," then it is one more example of the Pauline hesitation about fasting; J. Fitzmyer, *Jerome Biblical Commentary,* (Englewood Cliffs: Prentice-Hall, 1968, ed. by R. Brown *et al.*) II, 49:27 (p. 244); H. D. Betz, *Galatians* (Philadelphia: Fortress, 1979) 217–219; cf. also Col 2:16.

CHAPTER NINE

The Meaning of Fasting
in the New Testament

Summarizing the results obtained in the previous chapters, we arrive at the following conclusions:

THE BRIDEGROOM

The central message of the New Testament is love, the love that God has for us by sending his only-begotten Son, and the love that we have for him with our whole heart and soul and mind and strength, and for one another as for ourselves. It is a single fabric of love, from God to us through Jesus the Messiah, and from us to God through him. In Jesus God loves us, and we love God. He is the center of revelation and redemption, the fulfillment of the promise. Love is his message, and "bridegroom" is his symbol, a combination of love, joy, festivity, fulfillment.

Whatever meaning fasting may have in such a context, its place is certainly subordinate. Love comes first. This is the primary parameter in determining the value of fasting—fasting is good if it promotes and serves love, it is bad if it does not. Fasting is authentic if performed as a sign and as a means of growth in love; it is barren and leads to death if taken out of this context. This truth is expressed in a variety of ways in the New Testament, but the most significant is the image of the bridegroom. The disciple of Jesus, the Christian, is a wedding guest and experiences the joy of the presence of Jesus the bridegroom. This joy is a spiritual one and arises from nearness to Jesus. He is the fulfillment of the ages, the mediator of the Father's presence, the illuminator of truth at its deepest, the one who opens our eyes to divine revelation, who gives us courage and hope. The nearness is not physical; it is spiritual, but still very real.

Jesus dramatized the significance of his presence by dispensing his disciples from the many fasts that characterized John the Baptist and the Pharisees, not in order to eat, drink, and be merry, but in order to share a fellowship of love and conviviality with tax collectors and sinners, with the outcast and rejected, those most starving for love and acceptance and yet most deprived of it. The contrast between the fasting Pharisees who fear to touch a tax collector lest they become unclean, and Jesus, who calls Levi to be an apostle and who pleasantly dines in the company of sinners, is striking. It is understandable that some commentators, viewing this scene, feel that Jesus abolished fasting altogether! But that is too shortsighted. The reality of acceptance and love is a complex one, and the need of purification of selfishness and egotism in an effort to reach out to others is ever present. Fasting has its place in this process of purification and outreach, but it must be rooted in love, coming from it and leading toward it.

Jesus, besides revealing the primacy of love, came also to bring eschatological fulfillment, eternal happiness. The final, unending wedding feast is beyond the grave, and the perfection of love and joy which dispenses completely from fasting is found only there. Here on earth we are still on pilgrimage, on the way toward the fullness of life and love, beset by temptations and weakness, cravings and selfishness, rationalizations and hardness of heart. The need for discipline, courage, and effort is palpable, and fasting is a powerful means of bringing this about.

THE DESERT

Nothing is more terrifying to man than isolation and loneliness, the sense of helplessness one feels when alone in the face of danger which, if demonic, is all the more perilous and threatening. The Gospels of Matthew and Luke present Jesus not only as the bridegroom, eating with tax collectors and sinners, but also as led by the Spirit into the desert where he fasted and where, alone and hungry, he was tempted by the devil.

Centuries before, the Israelites had been in that desert, uprooted from the painful yet secure sojourn in Egypt, hungry for the leeks and fleshpots they had left behind, tired of manna and fearful of divine guidance, rebellious in their hearts against the Lord, unwilling to give him their faith and trust. They taunted his servant Moses and accused him of having led them into the desert to die (Ex 17:3). Yet these very Israelites were the chosen people, God's special children (Ex 4:22; Dt 32:6; Hos 11:1) who had seen the divine glory and the signs wrought in Egypt and in the wilderness (Nm 14:22). Nevertheless they tested the Lord and forgot his mighty works (Ps 106:13). The reality of human weakness, the temptation to give up on God in times of difficulty is poignantly expressed. Through his fasting and hunger Jesus participated in this weakness and temptation, but through his fidelity as Son of God he overcame it, and by fasting with him in the desert we too can overcome it.

As an evocation of Jesus in the desert, fasting can also allow us to grasp the sublimity of his answer to the devil: "It is written, Man shall not live by bread alone!" In the midst of hunger, fear, and deprivation of fasting a new horizon appears. We become aware that the things of the spirit are superior, that we must not limit our concerns only to the cares of this world, to the accumulation and enjoyment of temporal goods. We gradually realize what it means to live by every word that comes from the mouth of God: to allow ourselves to be guided by whatever is involved in the interpretation of his will, of our vocation. The grand design of an omnipotent Creator, Redeemer, and Sanctifier meets with our enthusiastic approval, and we are ready to give ourselves totally to his service. His word is our life and salvation. Indeed, man does not live by bread alone.

There is still a further dimension to fasting in the desert, one not immediately apparent but nevertheless important: penance. Jesus was sinless, but the Israelites were not. They had transgressed the commands of the Lord and had hardened their hearts. They needed to be purified and to repent. Dt 8:2–6, which this scene brings to mind, ends with the admonition: "Know then in your heart that as a man disciplines his son, the Lord your God disciplines you. So you shall keep the commands of the Lord your God, by walking in his ways and by fearing him." A *metanoia,* a change had to take place. They had to be transformed from rebellious murmurers into faithful servants. The hardships undergone in the desert were a divine pedagogy to bring about this conversion. Jesus, the faithful Son of God, is presented as reliving the desert experience of the Israelites, and so the motif of penance in his fast is at least implied. If there is a further allusion to the forty-day fast of Moses in the desert as a vicarious penance (Dt 9:18), then the relationship between fasting and penance is emphasized even more.

ALMSGIVING, PRAYER, AND FASTING IN SECRET

The linkage of fasting to prayer and almsgiving is a most fruitful one. Fasting intensifies prayer. It brings us before God in our totality and helplessness and humbly asks his omnipotence to intervene. Not without cause did the early Church complete Mk 9:29, "this kind cannot be driven out by anything but prayer—and fasting"! In difficulty and desperation fasting says more than words, for it proclaims to God our inability and weakness, and the seriousness of our petition. St. Augustine said, "Do you wish your prayer to fly toward God? Give it two wings: fasting and almsgiving."[1]

The relationship of fasting to almsgiving is equally important. Fasting allows us to deprive ourselves in order to help someone else; we can give the money we save by fasting to the poor and starving. This was emphasized particularly by the Fathers and Doctors of the Church, and is in vogue once again today. Many local churches urge their parishioners to fast during Lent and to give the money they would otherwise have spent into a collection for the needy. The "Rice Bowl" movement has been supported enthusiastically in many parts of the United States.

The value of fasting in relation to the poor is, however, greater than its merely being a source of alms, money that would otherwise have been used for oneself. Fasting opens our hearts toward our neighbor. It gives us solidarity with the hungry, the weak. We know what it feels like not to eat. We face the fear of starvation. We can sympathize with those for whom this is not just a chosen act but a terrifying way of life. Perhaps tomorrow there will be no food. We can be led to help others, not grudgingly, but with zeal and compas-

---

1. St. Augustine, *Enarr. in Ps 42,* PL 36, 482.

sion. We want to feed all the starving, taking nothing for ourselves. This is growth in fellowship, real self-investing, Christ-like love.

The teaching of Jesus about fasting, prayer, and almsgiving contains a serious warning: no vanity, lest that be our only reward! We are to fast "in secret," before the sole gaze of our loving heavenly Father! If we act exclusively for him, he will grant us a reward that surpasses everything else: a more intimate union with him that will never end.

HUMILITY

The "exemplary story" of the Pharisee and tax collector praying in the Temple is most significant: the destructive corrosiveness of pride and its total rejection by God is dramatically portrayed. Of what value is fasting, even twice a week, when done in a spirit of self-righteousness and disdain for others not quite as pious? Absolutely none! God looks at the heart and not at the list of good works performed. This judgment is a wonderful guide for the spiritual life.

Those who exert themselves strenuously in the practice of ascetical mortification may notice others not as fervent, and may be tempted to look down on them. They may also be led to consider their arduous spiritual exercises as particularly valuable and meritorious. Let them beware lest they be rejected as was the Pharisee; they ought to realize that no one has the right to disdain his or her neighbor. All of us are sinners, but God will forgive and sanctify each one who kneels down and in his or her heart humbly prays, "O God, be merciful to me, a sinner." Fasting can lead to pride and to presumption; the story of the Pharisee and tax collector warns against both.

FEAR OF DEMONS: MOTIF EXCLUDED?

In many cultures, including the Greek, fear of being infected by evil spirits gave rise to the avoidance of certain foods which were considered to be particularly open to their malevolent influence, such as wine, beans, meat, etc. Total fasting on certain occasions, especially in times of mourning, had the same basic motivation; it was a means of expressing one's sorrow, but it also served to defend oneself against possible harm from the spirit of the deceased.

Mourning rites in Israel included fasting (1 Sam 31:13; 2 Sam 1:12) and probably had a similar origin, though the texts no longer refer to the fear of being harmed by the departed spirit, unless one might see an allusion to this in the account of Saul's fast before consulting the shade of Samuel with the help of the witch of Endor (1 Sam 28:3–20, esp.20).

Perhaps this aspect of fasting is no longer valid in the New Testament. Jesus did not address himself to the problem, but his call to fast in secret, before God alone, may be taken to exclude reference to all secondary figures. Certainly Col 2:20–23, I Tim 4:3; 5:23 and similar texts polemicized against prohibitions of food; Timothy was urged to drink a little wine, in direct defiance of those who feared demonic contamination. The best rule to follow was that of 1 Tim 4:4f: "Everything created by God is good, and nothing is to be rejected if it is received with thanksgiving, for then it is consecrated by the word of God and prayer."[2]

---

2. H. Musurillo, "The Problem of Ascetical Fasting in the Greek Patristic Writers," *Traditio* 12 (1956) 1–64, esp. 19–23, points out that fasting because of the connection between demons and certain foods "explicitly at least, is extremely rare among patristic writers" but is nevertheless "prominent in the pseudo-Clementine *Homilies* and *Recognitions* . . . of the third century" (p.20). As in the case of slavery, the principles for abolition were given in the New Testament but it took a long time for practice to follow suit.

CHAPTER TEN

Fasting Today

In the light of the hermeneutical principles sketched at the beginning, together with the motifs provided by a study of the Synoptic texts on fasting, we are now in a position to present the biblical meaning and motivation that underlie the Christian idea of fasting today. The results may be stated as follows:

SELF-UNDERSTANDING AND LOVE THROUGH FASTING

In answer to the question "Why should I fast?" the New Testament responds, "As a sign of your love." If fasting is to lead us to a better self-understanding in our essential relationships—toward ourselves, others, the world, and God—then it must be carried out in the perspective of love; it must grow out of love and tend toward it.

In terms of relationship toward *self,* fasting acts as an instrument of purification, of penance, and as a test of faith. It is the painful renunciation of a legitimate joy, the pleasure of eating. It fosters self-control and is an effective help in becoming aware of our inordinate cravings and egotism. It gradually purifies us of our selfishness, the principal enemy of love, and thus nourishes the growth of love in our heart.

Fasting strengthens our inner independence from the many temptations surrounding us and makes us more capable of responding to the impulses of reason and generosity; it frees us from an over-concentration on self. As a penance, it is the recognition of past failings, of the many times we have given in to selfish desires and have cut ourselves off from others.

At a deeper level, fasting brings us to the realm of ultimate questions, those of life and death. It is the acknowledgement of our contingency and mortality, a facing of death, for if we were to continue to fast indefinitely, we would die. At the same time it is an expression of our belief in a future life, in a value that supersedes the pleasure of eating, the "reward" promised by Mt 6:18. It also makes us aware that "Man shall not live by bread alone" (Mt 4:4/Lk 4:4), that there is a whole world of the spirit to be discovered and explored, that the accumulation and enjoyment of temporal goods are not enough to fill the heart, that we have opportunities and obligations which far transcend the purely material and which bring far greater happiness and peace for they are in conformity with the words that "proceed from the mouth of God." Fasting makes us "hunger and thirst for righteousness" and gives us the hope that we will be satisfied (Mt 5:6).

As taught in the Synoptic Gospels, fasting promotes our relationships also with *others*. By joining fasting to almsgiving, Mt. 6:1–18 assured the Church that fasting would always be other-directed, that it would somehow be performed in the service of our neighbor, either directly, by giving to another the food or money saved by fasting, or indirectly, and even more profoundly, by creating a bond of sympathy and understanding for those who hunger, the millions who even today are starving to death. Fasting makes us aware of their pain and suffering, of the terror that they must feel in the uncertainty of food for the morrow, and it creates in us a strong desire to help them, to restructure the distribution of this world's goods so that all will have enough to eat.

In addition, fasting leads toward a better self-understanding in our relationship to the *world*. It acts as a corrective to the consumer mentality which looks upon the universe as something to be exploited. Fasting provides us with a philosophical distance, a pause for reflection, and teaches us to use the earth's resources with care and respect.

Finally, fasting puts us in a special way in the presence of *God*. We humble ourselves before him, accepting him as the Lord and Creator of the universe and of ourselves. Fasting is a witness of gratitude for the gift of life which is not of our own production and which we do not ultimately sustain. It is an existential manifestation of our dependence on God. We fast "in secret," uniquely in his presence;

we do not measure ourselves with others, do not disdain those who might not be fasting, do not become proud because of our self-control. No, our fundamental relationship is with God; we express our contingency and his omnipotence.

On this basis we approach him in prayer; indeed, we fast as an intensification of the essential meaning of prayer. We humbly petition God in his mercy, power, and paternal love to come to our assistance. We ask him in effect: "Do you want us to die? Help us!" It is a prayer said in confidence, with the presence of Jesus in the desert before our eyes. He does not turn stones into bread for he waits with filial trust upon the will of his Father. His words about faith in the Father's goodness have a special meaning in the context of fasting: "What man of you, if his son asks him for bread, will give him a stone?" (Mt 7:9). A human father does not wish his son to die, and so gives him bread, the food he needs; our heavenly Father will do so in an even greater way. Jesus himself, according to Mt 15:32–39 par, had compassion on those who had not eaten for three days and fed them miraculously, a symbol of his willingness and power to fulfill their deeper spiritual needs, especially through the Holy Eucharist.

The weakness of hunger which leads to death brings forth the goodness and power of God who wills life. Here there is no extortion, no magic attempt to force God's will. We merely look with confidence upon our heavenly Father and through our fasting say gently in our hearts: "Father, without you I will die; come to my assistance, make haste to help me."

FASTING, OLD AND NEW

Fasting is an item of that delicate question of continuity and difference between Judaism and Christianity. Jesus brought something new into existence, namely his divine, Messianic presence, and everything in the Gospels, including fasting, is touched by it. There is something new, something specifically Christian, to fasting, and yet, like the Ten Commandments and many other religious insights of Judaism, it is in continuity with what went before.

The Old Testament is accepted in the Church as the inspired word of God. The profound teaching it contains about fasting, especially in the prophets, is certainly still valid today. The New Testament does not intend to present a complete and detailed doctrine about fasting; it presupposes that of the Hebrew Scriptures, and makes only such changes as are directly related to the Person of Jesus and his mission.

As the bridegroom (Mk 2:19a), Jesus pointed out that there is a certain relativity to fasting: it is not compatible with final, eschatological fulfillment. It is not the essential Christian commandment; other things are more important. In his table-fellowship with tax collectors and sinners Jesus showed the primacy of love that reaches out to all, even the most abandoned and despised. At the same time, by dispensing his disciples from the fasts popular among the Pharisees and disciples of John, and by introducing the image of the bridegroom, Jesus gave a proleptic witness to the joy and glory that were to come.

Christian fasting is related also to the cross of Jesus. This is alluded to in Mk 2:19a, and is stated explicitly in 19b–20: "The days will come, when the bridegroom is taken away from them, and then they will fast in that day." In the early Church the Christians fasted each Friday as a mourning commemoration of the death of Jesus. But they soon saw that more was involved; it became a participation in his redemptive suffering, a special way of answering his call to deny oneself, take up one's cross, and come, follow him (Mk 8:34).

TRADITION AND CONTEMPORARY PRACTICE

Anyone who has studied the history of fasting in the Church throughout the centuries cannot help but be amazed at the great variety of attitudes and practices that have characterized fasting at different times and places.[1] There are very few constants; there is practically only one, the relationship of fasting to prayer and almsgiving. This was shown especially by A. Guillaume.[2]

---

1. For a good history of fasting in the Church, with concrete details about abstinence from meat, eggs, cheese, etc., and the gradual introduction of breakfast and supper on fast days, see the art. "Jeûnes," *Dictionnaire d'archéologie chrétienne et de liturgie* VII,2,2481-2501 (F. Cabrol,1926).

2. A. Guillaume, *Jeûne et charité dans l'Église latine, des origines au XIIe siècle, en particulier chez saint Léon le Grand* (Paris: Laboureur et Cie, 1954) 48,135,164–175.

Recent documents of the Church continue this tradition. Pope Paul VI, in the Apostolic Constitution "Paenitemini" of February 17, 1966,[3] which regulated the practice of fasting during Lent after the Second Vatican Council, wrote: "Liturgical texts and writers of all ages clearly show the intimate bond between the external act of penance and the conversion of the soul to God, through the intercession of prayer and works of charity."[4] The message for Lent by Pope John Paul II, dated February 28, 1979, also emphasizes this relationship: "Christ himself indicates to us in the Gospel the rich program of conversion . . . It is a question in the first place of prayer, then of almsgiving and of fasting."[5]

There is continuity in the Church's teaching about fasting, but there have also been many changes. The Apostolic Constitution "Paenitemini" gave a brief rationale for the changes: "The Church, attentive to the signs of the times, always seeks, besides fasting and abstinence, those new forms of penance which express its fundamental purpose most adequately for each new age."[6]

Perhaps the greatest change has been in the definition of fasting itself. As used in this study, fasting is total abstinence from food and drink for one day, from morning until evening. This is the old Jewish definition of fasting presupposed in the whole Old and New Testament. In stark contrast to this, but in conformity with the recent practice in the Church, "Paenitemini" considers fasting as meaning one full meal a day, with a light breakfast and supper.[7]

In spite of the changes in the concrete practice of fasting in the Church throughout the centuries, there has always been a desire to remain faithful to the Gospels. At times the Church has emphasized different aspects of the biblical text, but the concern was the same, namely to mediate to each new age the perennial message entrusted to it by Jesus. This brings us to the last point, the normative character of the New Testament.

---

3. Paul VI, "Constitutio Apostolica 'Paenitemini,' " *Acta Apostolicae Sedis* 58(1966):177–198.

4. *Ibid.,* 181.

5. John Paul II, "In the Cross the Call to Conversion. Pope's Message for Lent," *L'Osservatore Romano,* weekly English ed., 11 (March 12, 1979), 1.

6. *Paenitemini,* 181.

7. *Ibid.,* 184.

THE NORMATIVE CHARACTER OF THE NEW TESTAMENT

Recent studies on the different types of morality found in the New Testament have brought us a step closer toward elucidating the vexing problem of the extent to which the New Testament is a norm for Christian behavior.[8] E. Hamel points out that there are several types of morality in the New Testament and that they correspond in general to the main stages of the growth of the early Church: the *eschatological,* the *categorical,* and the *transcendental.*[9]

Eschatological morality is that represented by the earliest period of the Church when the awareness of the inauguration of the final age was still fresh, when the Christians were few in number and still visibly filled with the power of the Holy Spirit and the desire to give themselves totally to the absolute demands of Jesus for repentance and faith. This type of morality is found especially in the early letters of Paul and the early sections of the Synoptic Gospels, which contain few concrete precepts; eschatological morality expresses the essential command of Jesus to "repent, for the kingdom of God is at hand!"

Categorical morality consists in the concrete admonitions and prohibitions which the developing Church, especially in the later writings of Paul, had to give in answer to the many problems that arose in the attempt to integrate the new Christian ideals with daily life as the Church was expanding and getting organized in Palestine, Asia Minor, Greece, and Rome. The specific precepts of categorical morality were often taken from the Jewish and Stoic morality current at the time. There is thus a certain continuity between Christian and non-Christian morality at this level.

In the writings of John we find a third type of morality, the *transcendental.* This represents a return to essentials and reduces practically everything to faith and love.

All these types of morality are inspired and form part of the canon. In trying to determine the specific note of Christian morality

8. Cf. especially E. Hamel, "L'Ecriture, âme de la théologie morale?" *Greg* 54 (1973): 417–445; *Readings in Moral Theology No. 1: Moral Norms and Catholic Tradition,* ed. by C.E. Curran and R.A. McCormick, S.J. (New York: Paulist Press, 1979).

9. Hamel, 431f; I. de la Potterie, "Le problème oecumènique du Canon et le Protocatholicisme," *Axes* 4(1972):7–20.

we must take all three types into consideration, as being complementary. We might be tempted to reduce Christian morality merely to the eschatological and transcendental types, but the concrete categorical prescriptions taken largely from the non-Christian world are important too, for they serve to translate the more general commands of faith and love into daily existence.

In Paul we find the eschatological type of morality transformed into the *kerygmatic*. This is a christological morality, centered on the interpersonal communion of the Christians with Christ and with one another in him.[10] From the kerygma of the salvific presence of God through Christ in the life of the Christian there flows the *transcendental* morality of faith, hope, and charity. Rational elements from the non-Christian morality of the time were then added to form the concrete norms of a *categorical* morality. Some of these precepts were transitory, such as Paul's admonition to the women of Corinth to wear veils in church (1 Cor 11:5–15), while others seem to be permanently valid. It is often difficult to distinguish between the two, but great efforts are being made to establish proper criteria of differentiation.[11] E. Hamel notes that Paul often joined a concrete norm to a motivation based on the kerygma.[12] The kerygma itself refers to the life, death, and resurrection of Jesus and to his abiding presence in the Church and in the life of the Christian. The more deeply a specific precept is related to this kerygma, the more valid will it remain for us today.

We may conclude, then, that the eschatological acceptance of the kingdom, the kerygmatic union with Christ and the transcendental norms of faith, hope, and charity which flow from it are always valid, and that the perennial validity of certain precepts of the New

10. Hamel, 435; W. D. Davies, "The Moral Teaching of the Early Church," *The Use of the Old Testament in the New and Other Essays. Studies in Honor of W.F. Stinespring,* ed. by J.M. Efird (Durham,N.C.: Duke University Press,1972), pp.310–332; V. Furnish, *Theology and Ethics in Paul* (New York/Nashville: Abingdon, 1968).

11. J. Fuchs, "The Absoluteness of Moral Terms," *Greg* 52(1971): 415–458, esp.418–422, reprinted in *Readings in Moral Theology No. 1,* 94–137; G. Strecker, "Ziele und Ergebnisse einer neutestamentlichen Ethik," *NTS* 25(1978): 1–15.

12. Hamel, 437.

Testament's categorical morality is to be determined by the degree of their fidelity to the fundamental kerygma.

The validity of fasting is judged ultimately by the same criteria, by the degree of its relationship to the fundamental aspects of Christian doctrine, by its ability to foster union with Christ in faith, hope, and love, and by its capacity to prepare us for eternal life.

Selected Bibliography

ARBESMANN, R., *Das Fasten bei den Griechen und Römern.* RVV 21, 1. Giessen: Töpelmann, 1929.

————,"Fasting and Prophecy in Pagan and Christian Antiquity." *Traditio* 7 (1949/51): 1–72.

BERTHOLET, E., *Le retour à la santé et la vie saine par le jeûne.* 5th ed. Lausanne: P. Genillard, 1970.

BETZ, H.D., "Eine judenchristliche Kult-Didache in Matthäus 6, 1–18." *Jesus Christus in Historie und Theologie. Neutest. Festschrift für H. Conzelmann.* Ed. by G. Strecker. Tübingen: Mohr, 1975, pp. 445–457.

BORNKAMM, G., *Jesus of Nazareth.* Tr. by I. and F. McLuskey. New York: Harper & Row, 1960.

BULTMANN, R., *The History of the Synoptic Tradition.* 2d ed. Tr. by J. Marsh. Oxford: Blackwell, 1972.

BURKILL, T.A., "Should Wedding Guests Fast? A Consideration of Mark 2:18–20." *New Light on the Earliest Gospel.* Seven Markan Studies. Ithaca: Cornell University Press, 1972, pp. 41–47.

CAMPENHAUSEN, H. Von, *Die Askese im Urchristentum.* Tübingen: Mohr, 1949 = *Tradition und Leben.* Kräfte der Kirchengeschichte. Aufsätze und Vorträge. Tübingen: Mohr, 1960, pp. 114–156.

CREMER, F.G., *Die Fastenansage Jesu.* Mk 2,20 und Parallelen in der Sicht der patristischen und scholastischen Exegese. BBB 23. Bonn: P. Hanstein, 1965.

CROSSAN, J.D., "Parable and Example in the Teaching of Jesus." *New Testament Studies* 18 (1971/72): 285–307.

CURRAN, C.E., and R.A. MCCORMICK, S.J., eds., *Readings in Moral Theology No. 1: Moral Norms and Catholic Tradition.* New York: Paulist Press, 1979.

DAUMAS, F., "Introduction." *De vita contemplativa.* Philon d'Alexandrie. Paris: Du Cerf, 1963, pp. 11–76.

DELCOR, M., "Un roman d'amour d'origine thérapeute: le livre de Joseph et Asenath." *Bulletin de Littérature Ecclésiastique* 63 (1962): 3–27.

DENIS, A.M., "Ascèse et vie chrétienne." *Revue des Sciences Philosophiques et Théologiques* 47 (1963): 606–618.

DUPONT, J., *Les tentations de Jésus au désert.* Studia Neotestamentica 4. Desclée de Brouwer, 1968.

——,"Vin vieux, vin nouveau (Luc 5,39)." *Catholic Biblical Quarterly* 25 (1963): 286–304.

FANIN, L., "L'interrogazione sul digiuno: Mc 2, 18–22." *Miscellanea Francescana* 76 (1976): 93–107.

FEUILLET, A., "La controverse sur le jeûne (Mc 2, 18–20; Mt 9, 14–15; Lc 5, 33–35)." *Nouvelle Revue Théologique* 90 (1968): 113–136; 252–277.

——,"L'épisode de la tentation d'après l'Évangile selon saint Marc (1, 12–13)." *Estudios Bíblicos* 19 (1960): 49–73.

——,"Le récit lucanien de la tentation (Lc 4, 1–13)." *Biblica* 40 (1959): 613–631.

GAIDE, G., "Question sur le jeûne. Mc 2, 18–22." *Assemblées du Seigneur* 39 (1972): 44–54.

GEOLTRAIN, P., "Le traité de la vie contemplative de Philon d'Alexandrie. Introduction, traduction, et notes." *Semitica* 10 (1960): 5–67.

GEORGE, A., "La justice à faire dans le secret (Matthieu 6, 1–6 et 16–18)." *Biblica* 40 (1959): 590–598.

GERHARDSSON, B., "Geistiger Opferdienst nach Matth 6, 1–6.16–21." *Neues Testament und Geschichte. Festschrift für O. Cullmann.* Ed by H. Baltensweiler et al. Zürich/Tübingen: Theologischer Verlag/Mohr, 1972, pp. 69–77.

——,*The Testing of God's Son (Matt 4:1–11 & Par),* Ch. 1–4, Tr. by J. Toy. Lund: Gleerup, 1966.

GERLITZ, P., "Fasten als Reinigungsritus." *Zeitschrift fur Religions- und Geistesgeschichte* 20 (1968): 212–222.

GOMA CIVIT, I., "Sous le regard de Dieu (Mt 6,1–6.16–18)." *Assemblées du Seigneur* 25 (1966): 33–45.

GUILLAUME, A., *Jeûne et charité dans l'Église latine, des origines au XIIe siècle en particulier chez saint Léon le Grand.* Paris: Laboureur et Cie, 1954.

————,"Jeûne, prière, aumône dans le monde moderne." *Assemblées du Seigneur* 25 (1966): 71–83.

HAMEL, E., "L'Écriture, âme de la théologie morale?" *Gregorianum* 54 (1973): 417–445.

HOFFMANN, P., "Die Versuchungsgeschichte in der Logienquelle." *Biblische Zeitschrift* 13 (1969): 207–223.

HUBER, W., *Passa und Ostern.* Untersuchungen zur Osterfeier der alten Kirche. BZNW 35. Berlin: Töpelmann, 1969.

HUGHES, J.H., "John the Baptist: The Forerunner of God Himself." *Novum Testamentum* 14 (1972): 191–218.

JEREMIAS, J., *New Testament Theology.* Tr. by J. Bowden. London: SCM Press, 1971.

————,*The Parables of Jesus.* 3d ed. Tr. by S.H. Hooke. London: SCM Press, 1972.

KEE, A., "The Old Coat and the New Wine. A Parable of Repentance." *Novum Testamentum* 12 (1970): 13–21.

————,"The Question about Fasting." *Novum Testamentum* 11 (1969): 161–173.

KELLY, H.A., "The Devil in the Desert." *Catholic Biblical Quarterly* 26 (1964): 190–220.

KÜMMEL, W.G., *Promise and Fulfillment.* 2d ed. Tr. by D. Barton. London: SCM Press, 1961.

————,*Theology of the New Testament.* Tr. by J. Steely. London: SCM Press, 1974.

KUTSCH, E., " 'Trauerbräuche' und 'Selbstminderungsriten' im Alten Testament." *Theologische Studien* 78. Zürich: EVZ-Verlag, 1965, pp. 25–42.

LEONARD, F., "Shared Fasting." *Clergy Review* 57 (1972): 210–213.

LEONARDI, G., "Il racconto sinottico delle tentazioni di Gesù: fonti, ambiente e dottrina." *Studia Patavina* 16 (1969): 391–429.

LINTON, O., "The Parable of the Children's Game (Mt 11:16–19 = Lk 7:31–35)." *New Testament Studies* 22 (1976): 159–179.

LIPINSKI, E., *La liturgie pénitentielle dans la Bible.* Paris: Du Cerf, 1969.

LIPPERT, P., "Selbstverleugnung als Lebensfeindschaft?" *Geist und Leben* 49 (1976): 21–31.

LOWY, S., "The Motivation of Fasting in Talmud Literature." *Journal of Jewish Studies* 9 (1958): 19–38.

MALONEY, G.A., *A Return to Fasting*. Pecos, NM 87552: Dove Publications, 1974, 27 pp.

MEREDITH, A., "Asceticism—Christian and Greek." *Journal of Theological Studies* N.S. 27 (1976): 313–332.

MOTTU, H., " 'The Pharisee and the Tax Collector.' Sartrian Notions as Applied to the Teaching of Scripture." *Union Seminary Quarterly* 29 (1974): 195–213.

MOURLON BEERNAERT, P., "Jésus controversé. Structure et théologie de Marc 2,1–3,6." *Nouvelle Revue Théologique* 95 (1973): 129–149.

MUDDIMAN, J.B., "Jesus and Fasting. Mark ii.18–22." *Jésus aux origines de la christologie*. Ed. by J. Dupont. Leuven: Leuven University Press, 1975, pp. 271–281.

MUSSNER, F., "Ner nicht erkannte Kairos (Mt 11, 16–19 = Lc 7, 31–35)." *Biblica* 40 (1959): 599–613.

MUSURILLO, T., "The Problem of Ascetical Fasting in the Greek Patristic Writers." *Traditio* 12 (1956): 1–64.

NAVONE, J., "The Temptation Account in St. Luke (4:1–13)." *Scripture* 20 (1968): 65–72.

———,*Themes of St. Luke*. Rome: Gregorian University Press, 1970.

O'HARA, J., "Christian Fasting (Mt 6:16–18)." *Scripture* 19 (1967): 3–18.

———,"Christian Fasting (Mk 2:18–22)." *Scripture* 19 (1967): 82–95.

POKORNÝ, P., "The Temptation Stories and Their Intention." *New Testament Studies* 20 (1974): 115–127.

PRINCE, D., *How to Fast Successfully*. Ft. Lauderdale, FL: CGM Publishing Co., 1976.

RANWEZ, C., "Le jeûne. Abandon ou réhabilitation?" *La Vie Spirituelle* 118 (1968): 271–291.

RÉGAMEY, P.R., ed., *Wiederentdeckung des Fastens*. Tr. by F. Kollmann et al. Wien: Herold, 1963.

REICKE, B., "Die Fastenfrage nach Luk. 5,33–39." *Theologische Zeitschrift* 30 (1974): 321–328.

ROBINSON, J.A.T., "The Temptations." *Twelve New Testament Studies*. Studies in Biblical Theology 34. London: SCM Press, 1962, pp. 53–60.

ROLOFF, J., *Das Kerygma und der irdische Jesus*. Historische Motive in den Jesus-Erzählungen der Evangelien. Göttingen: Vandenhoeck & Ruprecht, 1970.

RU, G. DE., "The Conception of Reward in the Teaching of Jesus." *Novum Testamentum* 8 (1966): 202–222.

SCHÄFER, K. TH., ". . .und dann werden sie fasten." *Synoptische Studien. Festschrift für A. Wikenhauser*. Ed. by J. Schmid and A. Vögtle. München: Karl Zink Verlag, 1953, pp. 124–147.

SCHNACKENBURG, R., "Der Sinn der Versuchung Jesu bei den Synoptikern." *Theologische Quartalschrift* 132 (1952): 297–326.

SCHOTTROFF, L., "Die Erzählung vom Pharisäer und Zöllner als Beispiel für die theologische Kunst des Ueberredens." *Neues Testament und christliche Existenz. Festschrift für H. Braun.* Ed. by H.D. Betz. Tübingen: Mohr, 1973, pp. 439–461.

SCHWEIZER, E., " 'Der Jude im Verborgenen . . . dessen Lob nicht von Menschen, sondern von Gott kommt.' Zu Röm 2,28f und Mt 6, 1–18." *Neues Testament und Kirche. Festschrift für R. Schnackenburg.* Ed. by J. Gnilka. Freiburg: Herder, 1974, pp. 115–124.

SPICQ, C., "I Timothée 5:23." *L'Évangile hier et aujourd'hui. Mélanges offerts au Pr. F.J. Leenhardt.* Genève: Labor et Fides, 1968, pp. 143–150.

STEINER, A., "Warum lebten die Essener asketisch?" *Biblische Zeitschrift* N.F. 15 (1971): 1–28.

STEINER, M., *Les tentations de Jesus dans l'interprétation patristique, de saint Justin à Origène.* Paris: Gabalda, 1962.

STRECKER, G., *Der Weg der Gerechtigkeit.* Untersuchungen zur Theologie des Matthäus. 3d ed. Göttingen: Vandenhoeck & Ruprecht, 1971.

————, "Ziele und Ergebnisse einer neutestamentlichen Ethik." *New Testament Studies* 25 (1978): 1–15.

TAYLOR, A.B., "Decision in the Desert. The Temptation of Jesus in the Light of Deuteronomy." *Interpretation* 14 (1960): 300–309.

THIERING, B., "The Biblical Source of Qumran Asceticism." *Journal of Biblical Literature* 93 (1974): 429–444.

————, 'Suffering and Asceticism at Qumran as Illustrated in the Hodayot." *Revue de Qumrân* 8 (1972/75): 393–405.

THOMPSON, G.H.P., "Called-Proved-Obedient: A Study in the Baptism and Temptation Narratives of Matthew and Luke." *The Journal of Theological Studies* N.S. 11 (1960): 1–12.

URBACH, E.E., *The Sages. Their Concepts and Beliefs.* 2 vols. Tr. from Hebrew by I. Abrahams. Jerusalem: Magnes Press, 1975.

VARGAS-MACHUCA, A., "La tentación de Jesús según Mc 1, 12–13, Hecho real o relato de tipo haggádico?" *Estudios Eclesiasticos* 48 (1973): 163–190.

WALLIS, A., *God's Chosen Fast.* A Spiritual and Practical Guide to Fasting. Fort Washington, PA: Christian Literature Crusade, 1969.

WARD, E.F., DE, "Mourning Customs in 1,2 Sam II." *Journal of Jewish Studies* 23 (1972): 1–27; 145–166.

WENNINK, H.A., *The Bible on Asceticism.* Du Pere: St. Norbert Abbey, 1966.

Scripture Index

Author Index